M000074387

THE GREATEST ADVANTAGE

Overcoming obstacles
from the perspective of
a 15-year-old foster child

TOMMY SIGMAN

Copyright © 2020 by Tommy Sigman

All rights reserved.

Printed in the United States of America

ISBN: 978-1-7343907-0-4

No part of this book may be reproduced in any form or by any electronic or mechanical means, including information storage and retrieval systems, without written permission from the author, except for the use of brief quotations in a book review.

Cover image by Jackie Wilson

Cover layout and design by Baj Goodson

Published by Tommy Sigman

tommysigman.com

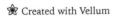 Created with Vellum

You cannot always control your external struggles, only your internal outlook.

— TOMMY SIGMAN

CONTENTS

MY STORY

As you may have guessed of a fifteen-year-old foster child, I haven't had a "normal" life. I am from a broken home, living out most of my childhood with my mom and little brother. I was constantly forced to move schools and homes—about every six months, in fact. In total, I was enrolled in thirteen different schools, lived in about fifteen to twenty different homes in six different states, all by the time I was fourteen years old. Needless to say, I became very familiar with bouncing from one location to the next, and not having much stability in my life.

Since my family was primarily focused on getting by month to month—just surviving—whatever our current circumstances were determined the most practical options of where we could live. Just as I would become comfortable in a certain area, we would up and move to a new location. Usually, we would move in with whatever man would and could support our family, despite any real depth of relationship between him and my mom.

This was the continuous repetitive pattern of my life.

My mom is a very strong woman who has overcome a lot

throughout her life, but she continues to deal with serious issues that probably started at an early age. For example, she was diagnosed as bipolar when she was a child, and has an extremely violent and angry personality. In fact, she once explained to me that she has a chemical imbalance within her brain and cannot fully grasp her own emotions; therefore, she gets angry or depressed rapidly and has difficulty trying to understand why her emotions are triggered so easily.

The older I got, her problems only seemed to increase as she became more violent and overly emotional. She was clueless as how to address her problems in a way that would allow her to grow from them, and her coping mechanisms were slowly destroying her. She would often turn to substances such as alcohol or cigarettes, which only worsened things. Her negative behavior elevated to a point where conditions left me with no choice but to begin searching for a new home away from her.

In doing so, I eventually sought out my dad. My relationship with him had always been a confusing one for me, growing up. There were periods of my life where I would see him almost every weekend, but then he'd be absent for a year or two at a time due to his addiction and legal issues, and that complicated our relationship.

Over the course of my childhood, my dad struggled with drugs, and due to my love for him, the reality of his being a drug addict—and the resulting consequences that caused him to miss out on countless moments in which I needed him—was difficult for me to grasp and accept. Plenty of people tried to point me toward the evidence that he was an addict, but acting as a naive child, I chose to ignore the red flags. My mom even used his drug use as a weapon against me, purposefully trying to turn me against him. Still, I refused to believe their voices of reason because I loved and trusted him. After all, he *is* my dad.

As far as I can remember, I had not seen him within the year when I asked to move in with him. By this time, reaching out to my dad was a desperate attempt to escape; I could no longer stand to be near my mother, nor could I handle the problems she was bringing into my life. We were living in Owensboro, Kentucky, had been evicted from our home, and were on bad terms with the landlords. Consequently, we were staying temporarily in my step-grandmother's house.

My dad was living in Texas, having gone there recently following a significant storm that provided many construction opportunities. At my call, he dropped what he was doing and drove from Texas to Kentucky to come pick me up. That night, we stayed at a hotel so he could sleep before we got back on the road; we were both genuinely excited to be together again, and I remember thinking things would finally be better now.

We stayed in Texas for a couple months and enjoyed it, but then the work began to dry up. As we searched for a new area with more potential jobs, it just so happened that a major flood occurred in Louisiana. Since that is the state we are both from, the decision to return to the place we consider "home" was an easy one.

To save on expenses and take advantage of the work caused by the major flood around Baton Rouge, we moved into my grandma's apartment in New Orleans short-term.

Now, understand this: her apartment consisted of one bedroom connected to a tiny kitchen and a bathroom.

Obviously, the apartment was crowded. In fact, we all three often slept in the same bed.

During our stay with my grandma, both she and my dad were constantly working, therefore forcing me to raise myself. I had the freedom to make all of my own decisions. It goes without saying that I loved the lack of boundaries, but I was not using that privilege and responsibility wisely.

Looking back, I guess it should be no surprise that this was the case. I was only in the seventh grade, attending a predominately Hispanic and African American school, and I was fending for myself. A large portion of the students I attended school with were either using or selling drugs; I did not want to become involved in this scene, already knowing what drugs had done to destroy the lives of my own family members, and I did not fit in.

Eventually, I fell in with the wrong crowd, yearning for acceptance amongst my peers in school. I was fighting frequently, and nearly got myself arrested because of my poor decisions. I was stealing, vandalizing, and running from the police, my behavior only growing worse until my dad informed me that we were moving—again. This time, we were leaving my grandmother's apartment for a small house outside of Baton Rouge to be closer to my dad's work.

The entire atmosphere of my new school and community was the exact opposite of the one I had just left. I went from the large city of New Orleans to a small country town that had little to nothing in common with The Big Easy. None of the students were on drugs (at least, not as far as I could tell), there were rarely any fights, and for the most part, everyone was welcoming and nice. It was refreshing! I made lots of new friends with truly good people who seemed to authentically care about me, and my life shifted into a different direction.

I still was at liberty to do just about anything I wanted at home, and I did love the freedom—but it came with a cost. I could do as I pleased, sure, but there was also that pesky responsibility of raising and taking care of myself.

Even though I knew my dad loved me, he wasn't making sure I had clothes, shoes, a properly cooked meal, or much of anything; I had to roll up my sleeves and find a way to acquire them myself. There were opportunities to work with my dad at different construction sites, and sad as it is, if I wanted basic necessities, earning a wage myself was the only route to getting them.

Because of my age, I was not paid much; but I had to get work where I could, despite low wages, and earn every penny, which transformed me into a more appreciative person.

However, the norm of these burdens became very upsetting to me when I compared my life to other kids' during this time. It was all I could focus on, and I failed to realize how much I'd been blessed with. Now, I'm beyond thankful for the situation having unfolded the way it did, because it resulted in my growth and appreciation for what I have today; but it wasn't so straightforward to me back then.

My lifestyle followed the same routine until I began to "wake up", as they say, and develop suspicions that my dad was on drugs again. I am still not sure what was secretly going on in his life at that point, but I steadily came to realize I no longer felt comfortable living with him.

Dirty people were invited over, and I was uncomfortable being around them. The house was disgusting, and my dad did not seem to have any desire to help me clean. I took to barricading myself in my room in order to escape the filth in the rest of the house.

I had lived with my dad for probably a year when I decided to contact my mom again. As you can imagine, I had a pretty weird relationship with her throughout the time I was away with my dad; I had left her, and it was not clear where we stood. But she made it seem as if the circumstances in her life had changed, and she even had allegedly discovered how to deal with her personal problems in a positive manner.

Taking her at her word, I explained my living situation and admitted I needed another place to go.

She came to Louisiana to pick me up at the beginning of the summer following my seventh-grade year. We drove to Florida where she was currently living with my little brother and her husband. I am not sure how long they had been staying there before I moved in with them, but they were living in a hotel room because they did not own a house at the time.

We lived in said hotel for weeks until we found a nice little house to move into not long before the school year started. This was probably one of the happiest points of my life, until I realized that none of it was real.

My mom had painted a false image of her true circumstances; maybe things were temporarily going well before, but it hadn't lasted long. She had not learned how to positively cope with her issues, so her sanity and happiness were soon exposed for the mirage they were.

I strive to be a person that rationalizes situations and seeks to understand someone else's viewpoint in an argument, but she does not. As she gradually became angry and bitter towards me, she was emotionally abusive. She would scream and absolutely freak out at me over the smallest of things that were not worth getting hysterically angry over. She'd make painful verbal jabs in order to make herself feel as though she was winning the argument, and in turn made me feel that I was less than her.

I grew tired of her anger, and was upset she had lied to me on that phone call from Louisiana; nothing about her had changed at all. Realizing I'd made a mistake in coming back to her, I became angry, feeling trapped. I decided I would not take her abuse, and began to yell and say offensive things to her in return.

It wasn't smart on my part.

However, in the heat of those moments, I saw no other option, nor did I care enough to find one.

Our battles escalated until she walked into my room one morning, gave me a cell phone, and told me I had three days to find somewhere else to live, or she was going to put me in a group home or otherwise place me with a different family.

I contacted one of my old best friends from Louisiana and explained my situation to him; he told his family, and I was blessed to have his grandparents pay for a flight from Florida to Louisiana. I left everything I owned behind except for a duffle bag of clothes, but the most painful experience was leaving my little brother again.

The original plan was for me to stay with my friend's family for a short time, just until I could find another relative to live with, such as my aunt. I was once again excited to escape the madness, but that lasted only a little while before complication reared its head.

My aunt became involved in some legal trouble, and there were no other family members with a suitable place for me to stay. No one was sure what to do with me, so I just stayed in my friend's home with his family.

"A few days" turned into about eight months. My stay there was amazing—I slept in the living room, but I was very well taken care of, ate well, had freedom, and was trusted by the family. They were sweet to me and became not unlike a family of my own. I truly loved living there, but I did not realize the full extent of how much my being there had put a financial strain on my host mother. She was an extremely hard-working woman, but she was a single mother with two teenage boys to support in addition to me.

It was during this time that I paid a visit to my cousin's home. I shared with him how grateful I was to finally be living in such a positive environment, with real support and acceptance. Ironically, it was during this same visit that I received a text from my friend's mom, explaining that she could no longer afford for me to live with them. She had been taking money from her savings to afford my stay, and could not take any more money out. I needed to find another place to live within the next couple of months.

Right then and there, it hit me: I was on my own again.

I contacted many other friends, trying to find any family willing to allow me to stay in their home, but it made me feel hopeless. I was a burden on others, and couldn't help it; I truly had no place to go.

You know, I have never failed to appreciate how much my friend's mom did for me, but during that time after her text, I could *not* understand her reasoning. I see now that she did not have much of a choice, but as I hung suspended in that awkward space between home and nowhere to go, I didn't get it.

Still, it was around this time that I experienced another shift, and I began to see life in a different light. I started thinking beyond surviving and focused more on thriving, asking myself how I could make my life better. I was determined to prioritize my education and work towards creating a better future for myself throughout the process of looking for another home.

At school, I was assigned an essay topic for English class, discussing a "big giant" I'd faced in my life. I explained part of my life story: how my mom kicked me out, that I was living with my friend's family and they could no longer afford for me to stay with them. The essay ended up becoming an opportunity for me to vent and get everything off my chest.

After I turned in the essay, my teacher soon came to me. She questioned me about what I'd written, and I admitted that I was in desperate need of a place to live. It was her responsibility to inform the school when she encountered situations like mine, and she did. This resulted in a meeting between myself and a social worker, after which I was placed in foster care.

Little did I know, my teacher had spoken to her husband, and after talking with the social workers, they wanted me to move in with their family. I had no clue what her home or family was like, but since I had no other options at the time, I obviously agreed.

Getting the green light to move in with them as a foster child was a long, difficult process. I finally settled in the summer after my eighth grade year, and I am living with the family to this day.

Moving in with them was a huge adjustment for me. They did not know much about me, and I did not know much about them, so the experience definitely brought a few bumps along the way.

They have two small children, and my teacher's husband is a pastor and in the military. They're very dedicated Christians and go to church more than any family I have ever met. Though they have lovingly taught me so much about God, and I am very appreciative of it, they value family bonding time to a higher degree than what I'm fully comfortable with. Furthermore, my new host family was strict compared to what I was used to, so my previously unlimited freedom became extremely regulated.

At first, I was angry and wanted to leave, but I remembered that this was officially my last option before having to live with complete strangers. There wasn't anywhere else to go, so I decided the only possible solution was to adapt and make the best of what I'd been given.

I had to learn to deal with situations differently and observe everything as an opportunity, rather than a setback or restriction, in order to allow myself to be happy.

For example, I was bothered by the fact that I was no longer able to spend the night at my friends' homes. I learned to stop viewing things like that as just a restriction, but rather an opportunity to focus more on myself and use that time to get things done toward the betterment of my future.

Throughout most of my life, I carried anger that never seemed to go away, along with other heavy emotions. I dealt with terrible trust issues, depression, hatred towards myself, and the false belief that life was unfair to me in many ways; but I have grown to understand that there are so many people in this world who would look at my life and instantly prefer mine to theirs, people who have problems that make mine seem insignificant.

Once I underwent this shift in thinking, I began focusing on the value in all of life, and became grateful for the life I was given.

But it wasn't all rainbows and butterflies, even after all I'd learned, and was continuing to learn. I had met someone throughout the process of moving in with my friend's family, and she soothed most of the negative emotions swirling inside me. She helped heal my anxiety, sadness, abandonment, and all the unfortunate issues caused by my past.

But then she decided she wanted to experience life without me. She texted me one day stating that she wanted me to become removed from her life, that she didn't need me.

It honestly destroyed me.

All the feelings that she helped take away, all came crashing back down on me, and I was miserable. I was forced to find new strength in order to keep sane and have any sense of happiness without her.

I believe God sent this person into my life, as she was a huge part of my growth for a year and a half. I admit that do not know where I would be walking in my faith if it was not for her, because it was at this point that I consistently began spending a lot of time with friends and growing closer to

God. While I became more grateful for the people around me, I also learned how to deal with being alone.

Along the way, I realized I needed a foundation for my growth. I was soon to discover the best possible foundation for my life: the love of Jesus Christ, which does not fail. Once my perception changed, and someone that had basically become my other half was stripped away from me, I gained a new appreciation for my life because I began to realize how much I was truly blessed within my new-found home.

Everyone has problems and obstacles that occur in their life, and I wanted to share my testimony as a tool to help others face their problems with a positive outlook.

You and I both know that just about everyone has dealt with some sort of pain in life, such as heartbreak or feeling lost. Honestly, I am writing this for myself in many ways, but I also want to bless others through the telling of my story. My aim is to help ease your struggles, reader, and guide you toward an understanding of how to deal with your pain in a productive manner.

That's what the rest of this book is about. As I am committed to the goal of growing as a person from each situation I encounter, and will not let my own story define who I am or hold me back from my potential, I have the same wish for you. The chapters of this book are dedicated to those who have been in negative situations similar to mine, but it's not just for them—it's for anyone who can possibly use the lessons I have learned throughout my journey to grow as an individual.

ADAPT AND OVERCOME

Now that you have a brief understanding of my backstory, let's get to business.

This chapter is the main premise of this book: learning to overcome obstacles.

Everyone goes through some form of pain in his or her life. I understand that I am only fifteen years old and still have my whole life ahead of me, but I have experienced genuinely deep pain in my short time on this Earth. I have been kicked out of my mother's house, been tormented by the uncertainty of not knowing where I would live or where my next meal would come from, witnessed family members using drugs, and I was left heartbroken by more than one person—all people that were extremely important to me.

I am not going on about my past because I enjoy reliving it; I am highlighting these facts in order to demonstrate to you that you can overcome anything with the right outlook.

You see, every single obstacle I have been through prepared me to adapt and overcome. I will not allow myself to be a victim in life; instead, *I will be a survivor*.

I have waged wars inside myself throughout my whole

life. I've mishandled anger towards my family, and the world, for putting me in a situation where I felt as if happiness was impossible. Similar to many of you, I did not understand why bad things happen to good people; but that is simply how life works sometimes, and we sadly cannot change that.

Some of us have not been dealt the best hand in life, and sometimes there is nothing we can do to alter the situation we were born into; but often we have the choice to address the situation as an opportunity for growth...or as an excuse for failure. Life is not fair, even for some of the most kind-hearted people there are—though I am a believer that generosity will be rewarded eternally when we choose to trust Christ.

YOU DO HAVE A CHOICE

Over the years, people have flippantly made comments to me, such as "poor kid", in response to the conditions around me. Consequently, I was convinced that I had no control over what happened to me. I was indirectly influenced to feel like I needed to just accept my situation as it was, which was largely not true.

For example, I did lack control over the decisions made by my family. But what I didn't see then was my ability to command my own mind. When I falsely convinced myself that I did not have any control, I was really feeding my mind an excuse for my state of unhappiness.

I eventually came to the realization that I would never be happy if I was allowing my environment to determine my emotional state. If I'm going to be happy, I have to make my happiness a personal choice for which I take responsibility. I cannot allow my issues or feelings towards my mom, dad, living situation, or anything else determine my state of happiness. It does not matter what I cannot control outside of my mind—my state of emotions, and the decision to choose how I respond to every situation, is and always will be completely determined by me.

With this truth firmly tucked into my heart, I can now wholeheartedly tell you that I am incredibly grateful for everything that has happened thus far in my life because I have a renewed perspective, and it's one that separates me from most people my age.

CHANGE YOUR PERSPECTIVE

Perspective is shaped through experience, and every family that I have ever lived with was vastly different from one another. While this could be seen as a problem, it isn't to me, because these differences supplied me with a wealth of perspective.

For example, my mom was an angry individual and was emotionally difficult to live with; however, she did try very hard to take care of me and supply me with the things I needed. I ate well, money was not as much of an issue as when I was with my dad, and I know that, deep down, she did strive (in her own way) to give me and my little brother a decent life.

Even living with my dad, when money was hard to come by, I learned a lot. I taught myself to be resourceful and use what I did have around me. Despite the financial struggles we faced, we were quite good at being poor, in a sense. While the standard of living in our home was not high, I learned that if I needed something, then I had to find a way to acquire it myself. That skill, in turn, taught me many valuable lessons that developed my character and work ethic.

Then of course, once I moved into my friend's house, his mom worked tirelessly to take care of us and bless each of us. She always found a way to provide us with what we needed, and even most of the things we wanted. Living there was probably when I was at my most comfortable, but it was also the worst for me because life became too easy, and I lost my sense of drive. I began to forget what the hardships felt like, and started to have less of an appreciation for how much I was being given, and how laboriously his mom worked to support us.

Finally, living in the home I am in currently has been the most unique. The members of the family are extremely close with one another and love spending time together. They do not have a ton of money, but they have enough to supply their two children and I with a genuinely good life. The parenting style is much stricter than I am used to, but they are probably the most loving and caring as well. I no longer possess most of the independent privileges that I had before, but there are also more opportunities that have come along with this family. Because the father figure of the family is in the military and is a pastor, he views parenting from a different perspective, and believes in good structure and discipline for his children, which I can respect. Despite the rare and temporary negative feelings that I may sometimes get from living here, they are one of the most supportive, and caring families I have ever met, and I am beyond thankful for them.

Through all the differences between these families, I adapted to suit the environment of each one. Each of the families were so different from each other, and I usually did not have much control over where I lived—only how I handled the new environments. During the periods of each major transition, my main goal was simply survival. But then I came to understand that, if I wanted to be happy wherever I was, I could not have the same expectations and hopes as I did for the previous home. I could no longer continue to hold onto the same values as before in order to achieve my target of survival and acquire happiness at the same time.

My new mission was adapt, adapt, adapt.

PAIN IS YOUR FRIEND

As you now know, I've been through many major changes in my life, and I can't honestly say that they were always easy for me. Dealing with so much uncertainty brought pain—pain that I did not know how to cope with. But I eventually discovered through all the hardships that pain is not necessarily a bad thing.

In fact, pain is your friend.

You should want to become capable of being comfortable while living in any state of discomfort. I am not suggesting to go out and purposely hurt yourself, but do understand that you cannot always control everything.

We all must learn how not to allow our negative circumstances to hold us back.

Moving homes and schools, dealing with my mom's anger and bipolar emotions, and witnessing the people I love deal with addictions, eventually became a lifestyle for me. It was not easy at all but it grew me, and I needed that pain to become a better version of myself.

I discovered that the more familiar and comfortable I became with a lifestyle consisting of such struggles, I could get through just about any challenge I encountered. The harder your situation is, the more of an advantage you truly have in the long run. A life of comfort and ease will not necessarily bring you to a destination worth arriving at. Pain is the ultimate drive that will lead to success; you just need to apply it and refuse to allow it to break you—because it is only through conflict that faith becomes a personal possession.

Until you have faced adversity and pain, your true worth —and faith in a God working in your life for a greater purpose—may remain a mystery to you.

The whole concept of adapting in this book surrounds the understanding that times will be painful, and learning how to take those hard times and turn them into something greater. Once you convince yourself that nothing can mentally break you, you will become stronger. In that place of understanding, you and I can become ready to take full responsibility for our situations, despite what other people may have done to factor into it.

Before I came to understand this, I constantly let pain hurt me and break me down, to the point where I wanted to take my own life. But by God's grace, I came to make a commitment to never allow myself to feel that way ever again, and to take complete control of my thoughts when they go astray.

Having power and control in your life truly does feel amazing. However, you cannot always control the external world and what happens in it—you can only control your internal outlook and how you go about every situation. Life is a battle every single day; it's full of tough decisions and habits in which control is key. So many people are confronted daily with questioning their self-worth, fighting against addiction, working extremely hard jobs that they hate to merely survive, and more.

My friend, if you are in a tough situation and need some form of guidance or resource to help you, then allow this book to aid in changing you and your life for the better. Use it as a tool to facilitate a change in how you view your situation.

One chief reason I wrote this is because, in the seventh grade, when I had to work a grown man's job to provide for my own needs, I wish someone would have given me a book like this. I needed this book when my mom would smash things and turn her anger upon me, making me feel hopeless. I needed it when the person I trusted most in this world—the one I then considered my closest family, the one I relied on for my happiness—exited my life, I needed this book to aid me in the process of mental recovery.

We could all use a lesson in refusing to allow life to break us. But we need to *develop* that mindset—cultivate it, nourish it, guide it as it grows. The difficulties you are encountering now shouldn't make you give up, but rather teach you how to become stronger.

People lose the battle against themselves constantly; do not let that to be you.

If you read this book and think you know someone that may need it, too, pass it along.

Because any situation can be overcome.

Pain can either break you, or elevate you by teaching you lessons. You choose to grow and potentially become the strongest version of yourself. You must conquer your mind to establish your own sense of happiness, and not let another individual's actions control your emotions. It *is* sad that negative things happen to good people, and it's okay to temporarily stumble—but never allow yourself to stay down.

You cannot always control the external world, just your internal outlook.

LEARN TO DEAL WITH YOUR PAIN

You already know how pain can be a positive thing and even be necessary for development, so let's take this chapter to unpack how to correctly and incorrectly use your pain to become a better version of yourself.

There are countless approaches to choose from when it comes to dealing with our problems, and I believe the ones we choose ultimately dictate outcome.

Believe me when I tell you that I understand what it's like to store away all your emotions because you believe no one else will truly understand what you are going through. I know what it's like to cry yourself to sleep because uncertainty looms overhead. I'm well-acquainted with the fear behind questions such as "where am I going to live?", or wondering if someone you care for deeply is planning to walk out of your life. I've been abandoned. I've spent large portions of my life drowning in loneliness, feeling hollow on the inside.

Whether you are my age or older and more experienced than me, we've all been hurt in some way. In turn, we've all fallen prey to that moment of "what now?", of not knowing exactly how to move forward—because to struggle is to be human.

But I want you to know that you *can* move forward.

Growing up, I discovered some spectacular coping mechanisms that allowed me to properly handle my struggles; I also discovered coping mechanisms that tend to destroy. By teaching you these methods that move you forward instead of backwards, I'm equipping you to get through whatever is holding you back now, or will one day threaten to hold you back because of future pain. Challenges in life will occur when you least expect it, and you should absolutely be prepared for them!

SUBSTANCES AND BAD INFLUENCES

It seems that, when people are experiencing pain, they almost immediately search for something that will ease the suffering. People may work out, focus on goals and acquiring success, listen to positive videos or music, spend time with the people they love, express their emotions on paper, etc. These are all examples of positive ways to wrestle with your problems, and may grow you beyond the inciting incident of your pain.

However, many of the coping methods which people more often choose typically result in leaving a person more damaged than by the original problem. The way we deal with a situation is everything, and the choices we make dictate how much stronger we become moving forward.

Turning to substances such as drugs, alcohol, and even cigarettes will only send your life sliding downhill. Slowly, perhaps, but slow is a pace, not a lack of motion. Pain is temporary, my friend, and will eventually fade away. The struggles you are dealing with now may or may not affect you in a week, month, or possibly a year; however, if they continue to affect you, adding substance abuse to the problem will just develop into more issues and won't allow you to heal.

Substance addiction leads to so many terrible paths that can cause your life to become a living hell. I won't lie to you —I'm *scared* of drugs and alcohol because I am aware of how much they affect their consumers. Certain people have very addictive personalities, and may become addicted to whatever will give them temporary excitement or happiness; and an addictive personality is genetic. I know myself and my family well enough to understand how easily I could fall into an addiction if I were ever to experiment, and that terrifies me.

A strong role model and mentor in my life once explained to me that if I never allow myself to experiment with substances, I cannot become addicted—and that advice doesn't apply only to me. I know this will fall on deaf ears for many, but I want to assure you that I am not suggesting that, as an adult over the legal drinking age, you can never occasionally drink; rather, I recommend that you hold yourself accountable while doing it, and that you regulate how much you intake.

That being said, I *am* also saying not to drink or turn to substances as an attempt to pull yourself out of a hard time, because *it does not work*.

I can't even begin to explain just how heartbreaking it is when someone you love is battling an addiction. Pain is usually temporary and beatable; addiction, though, is a constant, everyday battle to quit, and will ruin your life, as well as hurt the people around you.

Maybe you know someone who has used substance abuse as an escape for their problems, or perhaps you've been down this road yourself. It's ugly, right? And once addiction has its hooks in you, it can take you down fast. I am no expert, nor can I give professional counsel on how to defeat your addiction—but I'm all too aware of the extent to which it can ruin someone forever, and I can certainly caution you against that.

So many young people drink and smoke, viewing it as exciting, but they do not fully understand what they are doing to their bodies, or potentially to their future. It may be an exhilarating thrill in the moment, but you shouldn't deny the reality of what most often follows these habits.

I strive to spend my time away from substances because I do not ever want to fall into the same trap my family did. I refuse to allow anything control over my life, and I hope you will, too. Avoid being around people that make poor decisions, because those people will only hold us back, and we do not want to surround ourselves with temptations.

If you are on the destructive path of substance abuse, and now want to fully commit to changing your life for the better, shift your strategy to avoiding anyone that is even *possibly* choosing substance abuse, or making decisions that could lead in that direction. Don't let these people be an influence in your life. And this does not only refer to substance use; in general, it is best to surround yourself with people who bring out the best in you.

Obviously, nobody intends to become a drug addict; but pure intentions do not stop addiction from occurring. Decisions that may seem insignificant now can lead to a dark future.

If you were to study any drug addict, most will explain that everything began with a small decision, such as the decision to drink or smoke at a party. People tend to justify their wrongdoings by way of comparing their actions to someone else's, therefore making their own deeds seem far less sinister. Yet the Bible states that all sin is equal, and I know this to be true.

Let's hypothetically say someone chose to drink at a party.

Maybe they're young, underage. They told themselves it was acceptable because they were not an alcoholic. "I have the capability to control how much I consume. Besides, it's just this once. What can it really hurt?"

But it's never "just once", is it? Let's say this person continues down this path, because "just once" turned into occasionally drinking at other parties. Other than the illegality of it, nothing bad has happened. It's not a big deal, just a little harmless excitement every once in awhile.

Then something very painful occurs in this person's life. They may realize they enjoy the care-free feeling alcohol brings, and before they know it, they're using alcohol repeatedly as a cheap tool to numb their pain. Once that person develops a habit of drinking in order to cope, they end up becoming an alcoholic. Maybe it took a few weeks, maybe a few years. Maybe they're thirty by the time it happens. Either way, they justify their constant drinking, perhaps by saying, "At least I'm not a drug addict".

They convince themselves it's not the most destructive thing they could be doing to their mind and body. The path of alcoholism is not very luxurious, and they may gradually desire a more powerful feeling of comfort during their state of pain.

Suddenly alcohol isn't cutting it anymore. They may experiment with smaller drugs, such as marijuana, and tell themselves that they are not a drug addict so it is acceptable; but soon that individual will experiment more, and eventually will not be able to stop the decline as it comes faster and harder.

And another life has spiraled down, down, down, all because of one foolish, yet seemingly tiny, decision.

Now, you may be thinking to yourself that this is extremely unlikely to ever happen to you, but you'd be surprised, friend. All decisions, big and small, lead somewhere, so make sure you consider where the decisions you make now will potentially lead in your future. Consider carefully the people you surround yourself with, and how they could influence your decisions.

Have you ever heard the phrase, "you are the sum of the five people you surround yourself with the most"? It's very true. During hard situations, people usually crave comfort from others to help them grapple with the circumstances; this is not always a bad thing—especially if you are surrounded by the right people.

I have made the mistake of investing in the wrong group of friends and being negatively influenced by them. Of course, at the time, I thought those "bros" truly had my back. But if that were so, surely they would have wanted what was best for me. But no. They cared nothing about what was in their own best interest, or mine; they were only out for themselves and chasing temporary excitement.

There have also been points in my life when I didn't have many friends and simply felt alone. Sometimes, even surrounded by comforting people that I loved, I continued to feel alone; I was so focused on negative or absent people that I lost sight of who *was* there for me.

Fortunately, nowadays, I have been blessed with a support system through friends and family that is infinitely better than anything I've had in the past. They have demonstrated regular interest in wanting what is best for me. I know I am important to them, and they have become beyond important to me.

But through my range of experiences, I have found that it can be better to be surrounded by no one other than God rather than be surrounded by a sea of people who are negative influences representing the dark temptations of the world. You must learn to use a state of aloneness as an opportunity to act from your own conscience and to grow closer to God, who will never lead you astray.

Every human being has a conscience and can understand the difference between what is right and wrong. I believe that your conscience is God pointing you toward the right path. When people ignore their conscience and continue making negative decisions, that little voice begins to fade away from their mind. Once people become comfortable with their sin, they slowly lose that sense of God's supervision inside of them. When you commit to sticking with the wrong crowd, you will end up making poor decisions, despite how your conscience is warning you. Once you have separated yourself from the path of Christ, the potential for a devastating future will increase astronomically.

MASTERY OF MINDSET

In order to combat falling into the traps mentioned previously in this chapter, you must develop a new mentality: that everything that doesn't kill you can be used to grow you in a positive manner.

Some people are gifted and develop this mentality organically as they trek though difficult experiences, while most others fail to see the value and allow hard times to destroy or severely damage their mindset. Some of the most emotionally strong and successful people out there have originated from a negative background, but still managed to develop this mentality—and it was their saving grace. They have conquered their mind and refused to let anything dictate their feelings or emotions except themselves, which is what everyone needs to do.

I am the master of my own thoughts and feelings, and so are you, my friend.

Everyone in the world will go through hard stuff at some

point in life, because pain is inevitable. You will get your heart broken, or lose someone you love, or be betrayed by someone you trusted, etc. The upsetting truth is that pain is part of our lives and we cannot completely avoid it—only be prepared for it.

And let me be clear, I understand that when something horrible occurs, especially if we did not expect it, it may break us temporarily. We may feel like the hard times never end, and life becomes hopeless. I believe it is perfectly acceptable and necessary from time to time to allow yourself to grieve and pour out your emotions in order to heal. People tend to hide their feelings because they do not want to be judged as weak or vulnerable, especially men. However, it is hard to grow as a person and reach a certain state of happiness when there are bottled-up emotions buried inside of you. The faster you learn to get the negative emotions out of your system, the faster you can become stronger and grow from the incident.

FUEL AND DISCOVER

Once the growing process occurs, you can use the hurt you encountered as fuel to become a greater version of yourself than you ever were. You may discover and develop a better understanding of yourself. I, for one, discovered my passion for writing, and grew much closer to my friends and family; but it took being abandoned by the people closest to me to discover who I really was. In the process, I also discovered who my true friends were, and who was merely pretending.

The best way to heal from loss is to focus on and discover things about yourself. I decided I wanted to write this book and help as many people as possible because helping others and being around people that I love is what brings me genuine happiness. If you want to become stronger, use the hard times as a key to search for and find yourself; use diffi-culties as fuel to follow your passions, and strive to become a better version of yourself.

People tend to cope their way through tough times based on what they witness in the environment around them. Everyone subconsciously watches those nearby, and it really does have a critical effect on our own behavior and attitude. Remember that the way you choose to handle your issues must be positive, and does not necessarily need to fall in line with what people around you choose to do.

End the cycle of perceiving struggle as a negative thing.

Instead, preach to yourself that struggle only grows your character and mental strength. Whatever does not break you will grow you if you choose to view it as a positive building experience.

So, yeah, it is okay to stumble; just don't allow yourself to permanently stay down—and don't ever give up.

ESTABLISH A VISION

CONSIDER YOUR PURPOSE

A good friend I consider a mentor recently gave a speech at school. He described the "why" in life, and explained why we must ask ourselves the reasoning behind how we choose to act and make our decisions. The key message of his speech was for everyone to find his or her purpose in life, and it influenced me to evaluate my own purpose.

I envisioned myself as the man I wanted to be in the years to come. As I imagined it, I wrote down the man's characteristics, achievements, and the tone he set in every atmosphere. He was older but also wiser, and I had to consider what actions I should begin taking now in order to become this future version of myself.

I believe that it is selfish to only be what you currently are, to never strive to live up to your full potential, to consciously decide not to aim for the greatest version of yourself. I have met so many talented and intelligent individuals that were unhappy because they never chased after their dreams or fulfilled their potential, but rather just settled for a lazier, lesser version of themselves.

I am not implying that you should expect perfection, because you would be lying to yourself; no one is perfect, nor ever will be, because perfection is impossible. There is only one exception to this rule, and that was the life of Jesus Christ. Every human being will make mistakes from time to time because sin is part of our nature, and we cannot change that.

However, improvement is always obtainable, and everyone should strive for the betterment of themselves. We are all meant to achieve a purpose in this world—we just tend to interfere with that purpose. No one exists on this Earth only to waste away: make the decision to live rather than just survive. Sure, it's much easier to "get by" rather than flourish, but that will not provide you with true happiness. This common "getting by" mentality is established through the desire for security and practicality; but the work of envisioning something that may lead you to an extraordinary future is so much better!

EMBRACE HARD CHOICES

Scientific statistics have demonstrated that the chances of a human being born is one in four trillion. *Wow!* Let that sink in, friend. Because babies are born everyday across the globe, right? Tons of them! Yet people continue to refuse to take a chance on their dreams because the chances of success are supposedly too slim. That blows my mind! I believe that, the moment we are born, we are blessed with an opportunity to make the most of our time on Earth.

I have grown up around an absurd amount of people with no motivation or direction whatsoever regarding their future. The truth is, most folks simply live day by day based on their desire for temporary comfort that can only ever create a temporary happiness, if any at all. They choose to do what is easiest at the moment, and do not have a sense of urgency to unlock their potential because they're resistant to anything too difficult. In fact, everyone around me growing up lived for this temporary comfort. Experiencing a life lacking in direction led me to realize how much I wanted something different for myself, something more. This resulted in the ambition that I have today.

If you choose to surround yourself with people who have no vision or direction, they will drag you down. People with this type of mindset are exactly what I was referring to in the previous chapter. Be around people who drive you to accomplish tremendous achievements; because *their* dreams are so big, it could inspire *you* to dream big as well.

I understand how difficult it can be to exclude certain people out of your life. Maybe they have had your back throughout some very difficult situations, and you do not want to hurt that person. It is completely understandable to feel that way. Nonetheless, sometimes the people that claim to always have our back and perceive us as family are also the same people that hold us back the most from fulfilling our purpose. The only person responsible for the outcome of each of our lives is us; therefore, harsh as it sounds, we must exclude those with an absence of drive, or who feel as if everything is meaningless, or allow life to beat them up, the ones who constantly make excuses or choose to be weak minded, blame others for their issues, or anything of that nature.

Why be so drastic? Because we do not need their contagious negative mindset projecting upon us. If success and fulfilling your potential is your main goal, you must remove the nay-sayers from your inner circle and accept the possibility of feeling temporarily alone, and perhaps even guilty.

You may be thinking, "There is no way I can just get rid of this person that has had my back throughout so many obstacles!" I am not implying you should just immediately decide to cut someone out of your life that cares for you because of some easily fixable issues that person is dealing with. Respectfully approaching an individual and discussing the actions causing you to feel this way and then giving possible solutions *before* cutting them out of your life should be how our culture chooses to handle most issues. However, sometimes it is more damaging to hold on than to simply let go. As they say, you can lead a horse to water, but you cannot make him drink. Likewise, we cannot always inspire change in people, and it may take them losing us in order to come to some realizations and change their ways.

Of course, this route can be hurtful to those on the receiving end. They may speak negatively to or about you, call you unkind names, be angry with you, or any other combination of reactions. But having the right team around you is vital towards growing into the best 'you' and acquiring success. I would not have the perspective I do without having been forced to deal with the loss of relationships growing up. Each time someone exited my life, a new door opened for someone that wanted to be there.

I know I am very young and am still not fully aware of my purpose yet, but I have always known what potential I possess. Even so, I did not always know what to apply that potential towards, though I've consistently had substantial dreams and a determination to accomplish anything I set my mind to. But the bigger my dreams, the more people would tell me to be practical, assuring me how unlikely it was that I'd achieve said dream, and that I should give it up. They tried to convince me I should base my future around the concept of acquiring a realistic and secure job when the time came because that is what's normal. It seemed like they tore down anything I had my heart set on.

I wish I could tell you that I had an "I'll prove them wrong!" mentality, but I didn't during that time. I let their words destroy my dreams. It was my own family members that were falsely convincing me of these lies, and it discouraged me from chasing my passions.

Thank God I later came to my senses.

Obviously, we don't all share the same vision for our futures, so not everyone will understand yours, but that is okay. When people do not understand something, they typically do not appreciate it, and may have a negative outlook related to it. Simple-minded people do not appreciate big visions they cannot picture happening in their own mind.

It may be the people who love you the most that tell you not to chase your dreams. And don't be surprised when the same people that tore you down and insisted you'd never accomplish your goal later slap you on the back once the achievement is under your belt, saying they always believed in you.

No one can determine the path you take except you, and it is absolutely all right not to shy away from telling others your feelings on the subject. You only have one life here on Earth, so do not allow yourself to live in unhappiness, to not take risks. Some of the most successful and brilliant people in history were once criticized and called crazy, until they proved everyone that doubted them wrong.

STAND BY YOUR COMMITMENT

People who achieve their dreams and have the life that they desire didn't get it through luck. People may falsely believe that someone was an overnight success, but that person was most likely working at their craft for a long time before getting real attention from it. Success is developed through hard work, persistence, and patience. Dreams may take years to achieve, seeming impossible in the meantime, but almost nothing is impossible! Do not give up on the future you want because you are not seeing immediate results.

If the vision for your future is to spend life in a middle-class home with a lifestyle consisting of security and consistency, then there is nothing wrong with that. If you are settling for a lifestyle of practicality because you are lazy or scared to take a risk, then that's no good. When you have a beautiful vision but do not work towards it because you crave others' approval more, you are selling yourself short, friend.

Personally, safety and practicality are not my biggest desires, but there is nothing wrong with those. If you do not want to take chances or develop a big platform, but would rather just grow old with someone and live a happy and healthy life, then I totally support you. It does not matter what your mission is: find a way to achieve it. In other words, do not float through life like a dandelion tuft in the breeze, hoping everything will magically fall into place. If you want to be extraordinary, you must work harder than everyone else who wants the same thing and facilitate that future reality.

SET GOALS

No matter how big or small your vision is, you need a plan to work towards, referred to as goal setting. Writing down your goals gives you a clearer path to your destination. Make writing down these goals a habit. It is not a complicated process, but it is an important step. Vision without action is useless, a waste of the seed God planted within you; however, vision combined with execution can have boundless effects.

I suggest writing down daily, monthly, and yearly goals. I

like to give myself multiple goals throughout the day that can slowly lead me to where I desire to end up. My daily goals may only consist of one specific thing I want to accomplish, or a small list of multiple things. My monthly goals typically consist of one major thing I want to have completed, or the amount of progress I want to have achieved towards a specific large task, or multiple tasks. My yearly goals are my largest goals of all. My yearly goals list normally consists of the major things I will work towards accomplishing throughout the year, which will take me further along my journey of becoming the person I envision in my future.

Small growth and changes can be so important because everyone needs to start somewhere, but if you give up because you are not instantly seeing results, that means your vision is not large enough. If your vision does not change your life, and if imagining the outcome does not fill you with excitement, it will be hard to stay committed. I am not referring to momentary excitement, where a certain goal may sound fairly exciting or interesting to achieve in the moment; I am referring to an excitement that makes you thirsty to do whatever you possibly can to get to that certain point—something you can obsess over.

Obsession has a negative connotation, I know. However, there are certain obsessions which you may need to bring with you on the journey toward your ideal future. I am a firm believer that we should make God the number one priority in our life, as a close relationship with him will allow us to get farther into the journey we are striving towards. The more time we spend with God and prioritize him, the more joy we have throughout our life. There are missions and battles on this Earth that are too large for you and I, things we cannot face alone; but we can always get through any obstacle with the God that loves us and is worthy of our love and worship. After your faith, make your dreams one of your biggest priorities, and constantly chase after them.

LET GO OF THE PAST

If you have had a tough life or have often been in tough situations, allow your past to become the motivation for relentlessly pursuing a better life. I wondered for a long time why God allowed me to endure all I did, and I eventually discovered something: everything that happened in my life led me to valuable lessons through the hardship. I may not have gained my strong sense of responsibility and appreciation for my dad from living with him, if not for the struggles of living with my mom. I would not have been able to create so many positive memories and experiences with a friend that basically became my brother, if not for my mom kicking me out the second time I moved into her home. I never would have been blessed with this family that loves me and helps me strengthen my relationship with God, if my friend's family had enough money to allow me to continue living there. Upon consideration of my entire past, I believe it had to have been planned out by a higher power for a higher purpose: to help others.

I have not always had faith in God, nor did I grow up in a religious household regularly attending church. I always believed there was a higher power in this universe, that everything had to have come from somewhere. I was basically an agnostic, but was not committed to a search for answers. I cannot confidently state that I would have anywhere near the relationship I am building with the Creator if it was not for the family I moved in with and the influence of their outlook on life. I now want to fulfill God's plan for my life, and allow Him to use and strengthen me.

I understand you cannot always determine God's plan or

develop an understanding of why you are facing difficult times, but it is helpful to believe in a power higher than yourself in order to gain strength and a sense of reassurance. Whether you are a Christian or not, if you believe that only you have absolute control of your life and there is not anything guiding your path for a distinct purpose, setbacks are so much more difficult. I used to become angry for believing God was allowing me to go through such pain, but I realized my struggles only reveal His confidence within me. If you view every obstacle as God trying to teach you and shape you for His purpose, then your perspective changes. When hard times come calling, rather than only having "yourself" to rely on, believing that there is a Creator that loves you and is protecting you enables you to get through anything.

To recap, I've been unpacking a crucial truth: a large part of having a vision is focusing on the future and letting go of the past. I understand the pain from your past can feel all-consuming, but the more you dwell on the negative feelings of your past, you are allowing it to stop you from moving on. It's hurting you. When you spend more time focusing on the problem rather than the solution, you will not find the solution. Do not think of loss as an end, but consider it a new beginning.

Despite what you may be going through in this moment, things will get better. You may feel brokenness, loneliness, hopelessness, along with a host of other emotions. Just understand that *anything* can be for a higher purpose, can make you stronger. Use those negative feelings to find your drive and establish a better life for yourself. Learn not to hold yourself back. Trust God and His plan for you that everything happens for a reason. Most importantly, never ever give up on yourself or your faith.

CHOOSE GRATITUDE

HAPPINESS IS ALWAYS AN OPTION

In order to acquire happiness, one must decide to focus on the positive aspects of every situation and never allow yourself to fall into a trap of self-pity. Unfortunately, many people choose to direct their attention towards all the ways their situation is unfair, rather than accepting it and determining how they can grow from it. There is a common saying that "God will not give you more than you can handle"; however, I strongly disagree. I believe that God will absolutely place us in situations that we cannot face alone, but can overcome if we draw towards Him and allow Him to give us strength through situations that seem hopeless. God has the capability to restore whatever we have lost and allow us to understand how much we truly have.

It is challenging to be miserable when you are primarily concentrated on your blessings and constantly expressing gratitude. Nonetheless, every issue that you are facing is probably insignificant when compared to what someone else may be going through. It helps your perspective to be reminded that there will always be someone else who wishes they were in your shoes, despite how horrible your life may seem at times.

Happiness and gratitude are connected through what you compare different aspects of your life to. I have come to understand that I should not question why I am faced with the obstacles that have occurred in my life, while there are children younger than me struggling for survival in other areas of the world. On one hand, if I compare the situation I was born into with people who only demonstrate their best life on social media or with everyone who is more privileged around me in general, I will not feel compelled to express nearly as much gratitude or have a mindset that reminds me how blessed I truly am. If I choose to compare my environment with children in other parts of the world who would do absolutely anything to face my problems rather than theirs, I am constantly able to be satisfied with what I have. It seems to be common in my generation to develop a false sense of victimization because of the wrong types of comparisons people choose to make.

As I am learning to view life through this lens, I now feel beyond grateful because I understand what it is like to be in different shoes. I remember the feeling of not having home-cooked meals or a clean home, and now I am blessed to be able to experience those things daily. School can make us read every book and write every paper, but experience is something valuable that cannot be taught. Many people lack experience of genuine hardships in today's society, and there-fore do not possess nearly as much gratitude as they should.

You know as well as I do, there will always be someone who has more money, friends, family, success, romantic prospects, talent, and whatever else we may desire. We must accept this and appreciate all we have regardless, because everyone has strengths and weaknesses as well as blessings and burdens in their life. We must not allow ourselves to stew in jealousy or concentrate on the people who appear to have more than us because those thoughts distract us from bettering ourselves and expressing gratitude for our blessings. Do not ever look down upon people who seem to have less than you, either; choose to share your blessings with others and help the less fortunate, because it could have been you who was put in their situation. Remember that, as bad as you may feel life is right now, someone else always has it worse.

Perspective is the biggest factor in experiencing happiness, and it determines everything in your life. Perspective frequently changes, and is grown through acquiring more knowledge and life experience. Pain is one of the greatest transformers of perspective, and it can completely adjust one's outlook about everything. The expression, "the glass is half empty, or half full" is a good way to consider every event and obstacle. You can either view everything that happens to you in life as a trial trying to break you, or as an opportunity to help grow you.

Throughout the season of my life in which I was being placed in foster care and had a lot of negative emotions, I had someone that was by my side and helped me overcome so much just by her presence. She was the world to me. When she removed herself from my life, I had more negative emotions than ever until it got to the point where I became physically sick.

It was then, in utter despair, that I decided to use all the negative energy and hurt as fuel for self-development. I became obsessed with improvement. I fixated on my ambition to create such a positive impact on this world and the people around me that I wouldn't need to rely on anyone for happiness; nothing would interfere with my mission to help others ever again.

I began to constantly work on myself and spend time with the ones I cared about much more after my loss. My perspective and consistent gratitude allowed me to overcome one of the most painful experiences in my life, which had once felt like it was never going to come to an end. I could have allowed the situation to crush me, but instead, I was thankful for the situation because I knew it was an opportunity to grow.

I discovered through these hard times that there is a reason for everything. I talked about God's plan in the previous chapter because I believe in it. God may have taken that person out of my life for numerous reasons, such as the possibility that He has someone else set aside for me in my future, needs me to focus more on my goals, help others, discover my passions, etc. I was destroyed from the incident temporarily, but I cannot express how grateful I am for everything that occurred.

My advice to you is to never allow the hard times to break you when they are most likely happening for the betterment of your own future; God's always aware of what He's doing. Even if you do not buy into the concept that God has reasoning for everything, at least consider that, as Scripture explains, He can take that which is meant for evil and turn it to good.

I know there are situations where everything seems overwhelmingly negative, when things are so bad it feels impossible to find something to be grateful for. In those moments, just remember that there is always something to be grateful for, no matter what. Some of the darkest storms create the brightest rainbows. If you wake up and are alive, you already have something to be grateful for. When you complain about your life, all you are doing is focusing on the negatives and extracting from your own happiness. People do not realize that when they complain, they are only hurting themselves (and probably coming off as a negative person to the people around them). Whatever you choose to focus on determines your perspective, and your perspective determines everything.

If you come from a troubling past and want to grow into the strongest version of yourself, understand that your setbacks are a gift, and apply them. Life does not make exceptions for good people, and you will not grow from the hard times if you wallow in your misery, complaining non-stop.

My dad and uncle once randomly appeared at my house, in which I was staying with my mom and little brother. They brought a child with them that was only a little older than myself, but was not enrolled in school. We did not know much involving the child or his living situation, except his mother was being sent to rehab and he was in desperate need of a place to stay. My dad and uncle knew they were not suitable guardians at that time, so they asked us to temporarily take care of him. My parents were not close throughout my childhood, so my dad's act truly demonstrated how few people the boy really had in his life that were willing to care for him.

My mom agreed to let him stay with us because she did not want something bad to happen to this child. I didn't understand the full extent of his situation then because I was so young, but this child was one of the happiest and most generous children I had ever known.

Prior to this situation, my uncle had given me a little handheld gaming device with a bunch of games. I showed the new kid the device, and somehow he knew all the games I had before he saw any of them. He told me it was his. It had recently gone missing from his mom's vehicle, and it was his belief that my uncle stole it. I did not want to believe him because I did not think that my family would do such a thing; I was so young and naive. In spite of everything the young man was going through, he let me keep the device and all the games. He demonstrated to me one of the strongest examples of taking a negative situation and using it for good—to bless someone else.

I assume he ended up in foster care or moved in with a distant relative, but I will never forget him or his kind-heartedness. His act was very inspiring, leaving an impression on me. He did not let the circumstances of his life stop him from choosing to be happy or generous, and that is the type of mindset that everyone should develop. Whenever I begin to complain or think that my life is not fair, I think of him and his capability to face adversity at such a young age, and it inspires me to do better and become better.

The boy's act was a perfect example of happiness being a choice in spite of adversity. He made choices that separated him from the status-quo. We all have the choice to do something to improve the quality of our life everyday. Everyone has the capability to decide if they want to give to someone less fortunate than them, reconcile with someone, express gratitude, spend time with the people that they love, spend time with God, take care of themselves and their body, etc. Decisions are constantly being made, and our decisions are an ultimate decider of our emotional state and future.

DON'T PROCRASTINATE

One wise choice you can make daily for yourself that by extension aids in cultivating gratitude is to avoid procrastination. I personally have not always been so innocent of this myself, but it can stop you from accomplishing so much. Doing what is easier now to do what is harder later only causes stress and the feeling of dissatisfaction. I believe people tend to procrastinate because there is a missing sense of gratitude in their lives. When you are grateful for all the things and opportunities God has blessed you with, you will want to cherish and utilize those things and opportunities. I developed such a strong sense of ambition once my gratitude increased because I saw the many opportunities in my life. I cannot stand laziness and waste.

If your goal is happiness, do whatever is difficult now in order to give yourself more time later on to focus on other things. Once you develop a habit of getting difficult tasks out of the way as quickly and efficiently as possible, you will earn a sense of freedom. You may not always realize it, but the amount of energy that your mind uses to put something off is usually more than what it takes to complete the task. I suggest taking the time to evaluate your everyday habits and use of time, then decide what you need to cut from your routine to maximize time and get the most productivity and happiness out of each day.

I am discussing everyday habits and how they affect your happiness because this is a generation where people are subconsciously working against their own happiness through their actions. I am sure you or someone you've spoken with has struggled with a lack of energy, fulfillment, joy, liveliness, motivation, gratitude, etc., and just can't figure out why. Depression and suicide rates are continuing to escalate, and people are sabotaging their own mental state with their actions; procrastination adds to this. I believe the practice of gratitude follows with the practice of happiness, and happiness is vastly established through our habitual decisions.

An example of people's actions going against their happiness is when people cheat on their diet, cheat on someone else, give up on their workout routine, indulge too much in something such as alcohol, or do anything that causes them to fall short of the goals in which they were committed to doing or changing about themselves or their life.

One of the best feelings out there comes from accomplishing something you set out to do, despite the difficulties you faced throughout the process. When you do what you say you're doing to do, therein keeping your work to others or to yourself, there is a sense of feeling powerful and strong. People choose unhappiness by telling themselves that they have no control or self-discipline, when they really do. Don't allow your schedule to revolve around comfortability! This state of mental weakness is not something anyone was born with—it is learned over time. No one is born lazy or unappreciative; people act this out because it is either taught to them by other's behavior, or practiced through their habitual actions.

SHOW APPRECIATION

Lack of appreciation is one of the saddest choices people can make, and it's becoming more and more apparent through the apathy of this generation. Technology is flourishing, allowing people to become lazier each day with their made-easy lifestyle. We can literally order just about anything we want from our phone with a few taps, and it can be delivered to our home in a day or less. Most of us have access to fresh food and water on a daily basis. Can you imagine trying to make a sandwich two hundred years ago? Talk about hard! Everything is so much easier today than it has ever been for human beings, yet we are becoming more unappreciative as the days go by.

The upsetting truth is most people may never understand how much they have until they lose it. Once you become so used to having all your wants and needs satisfied, it is very difficult to have a strong appreciation for everything God has blessed you with because you do not understand what it is like to live without those things. I can promise that you will never be more thankful for water than when the water in your house gets shut off. Water is something that we use and take advantage of every single day, and there are people out there who would do anything to have consistent access to it. Imagine if we had to travel miles to the nearest body of water, just to boil it and go through a purifying process in order to drink it without it contaminating our body. People tend to forget how much easier life has become for us over the last century because such advances are what we have grown used to. I may not have had the best family or childhood growing up, but I know that I was born with many things and opportunities that put me in a position to constantly be grateful.

This philosophy applies to relationships as well; we may not realize a friend or relative's worth until they are absent. People tend to take for granted the most important people in their life. For instance, it's easy to forget that genuine and loving people are not a dime a dozen when genuine and loving is all you're used to.

When there is someone who truly loves you and wants nothing except the absolute best for you, make a point to show them gratitude often, because they may not always be there. I would rather lose someone due to a change in their own heart than live with the regret of knowing they left because I didn't appreciate them. Do not make the mistake of waiting for someone to leave and feel a world of regret before demonstrating how much you care for them.

On the other hand, if someone does choose to leave your life, allow it to be their loss; give that love to someone else who will not take it for granted. Allow loss to strengthen your relationships with the people who choose to stay at your side, whatever happens.

OPEN YOUR EYES TO WHAT YOU HAVE

Some of the world's most successful people come from backgrounds in which they were given very little. These people that originated from nothing understand what it is like to be at the bottom, and never want to be in that position again. Once you reach a point where you are at the bottom, climbing your way back to the top will feel greater than ever. Happiness will feel so amazing once you overcome depression. Food will taste so delicious once you overcome hunger or poverty. There will be such a strong appreciation for loved ones once you've overcome loneliness. Do not allow life to break you during your lowest state—appreciate the journey, and look forward to how amazing it is going to be when you recover. Especially remember not to allow yourself to be destroyed by a problem that's an issue just for right now, when this problem will not matter in years to come.

Let's go hypothetical for a moment, in which you have only one week left to live. Would your perspective toward all the good things around you change? Or would you be miserable in your near-death situation? Would you allow yourself to be jealous of insignificant items that others have that you do not?

The scary truth is that you never know when it may be your last week on Earth, nor do you know when it's someone else's. I like to imagine that you would desire to live your last week to the fullest. And since you don't know when your last week will be, live every week to the fullest. Choose to take care and appreciate all that you have now before it's all gone.

Take care of your relationships. If you ignore your issues with your family, partner, or friends, then they will not be resolved. If you care about somebody, preserve the relationship through effort. Anyone can choose to pretend not to care, ignore their problems, or avoid the person because those things require no effort. But giving effort is always more rewarding.

When I moved away from my mom, I realized how much she did for me growing up. I moved away from my dad and realized how much freedom and opportunity I had being with him. I moved away from my friends and realized how much effort it had taken to care for me. Once I moved to my current home, I grew closer to God and realized how many people in my life truly care for me. I did not always enjoy each of the different paths my life has taken, but they all happened for a reason, and I know I will always be grateful.

OPPORTUNITIES ARE EVERYWHERE

Did you know you're surrounded by opportunities everyday, everywhere you go? Most people fail to realize this, but every problem has a solution, and every situation can be overcome.

More often than not, restriction is a roadblock in our own mind; we decide we're trapped or hopeless when it's just a lie we tell ourselves.

Do not mistake unwillingness for lack of opportunity.

My philosophy is this: if something is not working, persevere until the solution presents itself. I refuse to give up until I've attacked a problem from every possible angle. People usually do not give up because of failure, but rather a failure to keep working at their goal when the path is long and hard; the journey from the beginning to the end isn't worth it to them.

SCHOOL IS A PRIVILEDGE

I understand a few fellow teenagers may read this book, and I want you in particular to know there is no excuse for failing school. School is one of the greatest opportunities we have as students of the world, and so many take it for granted. School isn't about having a social life, or proving how smart you are. Your grades are not a result of natural intelligence, but a reflection of your work ethic. School is meant to give young people a chance to establish a better future through hard work and persistence. We can even join a club, or participate in volunteering or tutoring to enhance and make the most of our educational experience. We are given an opportunity to work hard while we are young so we're less likely to become a slave to work when we're older.

It's okay that educational experience may vary between individuals, but nowadays there are nearly endless opportunities through school to accomplish anything you want. If you plan to go to college or trade school after high school, then taking your education seriously before you graduate is a must. In the United States, we are blessed with more opportunities than any generation before us when it comes to being set up for success. We have multiple platforms in the realm of social media, which connect almost every human on the planet. We also can obtain just about any information we desire through the internet in seconds. We don't know what it's like for our future to be dictated solely through family or location. We have the resources to accomplish anything, and we must take advantage of these resources in order to excel.

DON'T GIVE YOURSELF AN OUT

When you state you cannot do something, you are convincing yourself of this false statement. Stop giving yourself an excuse! No one *enjoys* taking responsibility for themselves; that's why we all like to blame our lack of achievement on something or someone else. But when we question how we can achieve something—rather than deciding we can't—we open our minds to new possibilities. Statements such as "that's impossible" or "I can't do that" only create mental limitations that stunt growth, but questions and optimism expand the mind.

Undeniably, some people are born with greater advantages than others; we can't change that. But when accessing opportunities is challenging, we better understand that certain opportunities may not come again. Being at the bottom of the totem pole can breed the determination to make the most out of the opportunities around you that many others may not have. People that start from nothing and become very successful take advantage of all available resources to reach their desired point of success. People that are given everything they need usually do not understand how much they can accomplish, or do not possess the determination to apply their resources to the fullest extent.

TURN LEMONS INTO LEMONADE

I was on the phone with my dad recently, discussing my living situation with my current foster family. He referenced the period when I formerly lived with him, commenting, "I decided that if I was not there and did not give you anything, you would have to work and figure out a way to get everything yourself, overall teaching you how to become successful." We just laughed and played it off as a bad parenting joke, but he was right. In my past, the lack of support when I needed something was one of the best opportunities ever presented to me. The challenge was an opportunity for me to either rise and overcome, or allow the circumstances to break me. I may not have been handed everything on a silver platter, but I discovered how to turn the adversity I faced with into something greater.

My social worker gave me a donated, old, slow computer to work on school projects and documents. As soon as I got it, I began to question how much use I could get from this janky old computer. When I chose to view it as a precious resource, while not ideal, it became invaluable. It was that same computer on which I typed the manuscript for this book.

I have come to realize everything in my life is an asset I can choose to leverage for good. I suggest assessing what you have in the environment around you, and determining how you can work with what you have to create new opportunities for yourself.

I bet you, too, have access to resources that you could acknowledge and take advantage of (in a responsible manner). Even if you have access to social media or the internet alone, there are so many opportunities available to you. All day long, people post ads looking for people with different skills and knowledge, some of which you may possess. Evaluate your skills, the resources surrounding you, and how you can fit it all together. Apply that information to make your desired future a reality.

People are a resource as well, mind you. Their experiences and perspective count as knowledge you can learn from to expand your own mind. And you never know what relationships you're building now that could be a major asset towards your future. Whenever I meet someone, my intentions are to learn something new from them or develop some understanding of their thought process in order to expand my perspective.

SUCCESS IS FOR EVERYONE

Every successful entity ever has had to start at the bottom and work their way up, and there is no limitation on how much one can accomplish. There will always be problems and adversity in this world; therefore, there will always be opportunities to create a positive impact. If you believe the world needs someone with your knowledge and abilities, then you must use every opportunity and resource around you to create that positive impact. Imagine how much different the world would look if everyone tapped into their potential/passions and did not allow themselves to settle.

The quality of your life is predominately reliant on you and your actions. Truly *anyone* can succeed in this world.

And to be fair, *success* is a word that can have ten definitions to ten different people. My definition of success is based on my perspective. I have succeeded in the aspect of conquering my mind, and not allowing anything I go through to break me. I have learned to overcome and use every obstacle as motivation and an opportunity to grow. I could acquire money, high status, wealth, power, respect, but I would argue it is hard to qualify those things as proper demonstrations of success when it is possible to lose each of those things.

My character is not defined by money, respect, or materialistic items, but rather who I am internally. The way I treat others, my ability to overcome adversity, and my connection with the Lord is what defines success by my standards. Those are three things that cannot be taken anyway by anyone else.

I have not reached my potential by a long-shot, but I believe I'm walking the path of success. And good news: *anyone* can do the same.

It does not matter who you are, where you come from, your ethnicity, family background, past, or any other aspect in your life to determine how much you can grow, and how much success you can acquire. Remember, despite any adversity you face, take advantage of the resources around you. Obstacles don't have to break you; instead, let them be an opportunity to grow and strengthen you.

MAKE THE DIFFERENCE

UNIVERSAL GROUND

Whoever you are and whatever you have gone through, if you're human, I know you desire to love and be loved by others. Everyone has emotions, and everyone desires to experience a sense of love and trust with at least one person. Sometimes the best remedy to our suffering is to help cure someone else's by expressing the love that we desire for ourselves.

Somehow, my generation seems to have created a culture of people who hide their true feelings, or act as if they do not possess emotions at all. It's common, too, to act as if no one's opinion outside our own has value. In truth, everyone values *someone's* opinion, despite what we may tell ourselves. Everybody desires love, trust, companionship, etc. associated with opening your life up to other individuals in some form of vulnerability and intimacy. Of course, it is absolutely possible to come to a point where you can ignore *most* people's feelings towards you, but that does not mean you do not care about *anyone's* feelings. Our brains are wired for us to be social creatures, and it would be unnatural for someone to not care the slightest amount if they were not loved or accepted.

A poor decision humans constantly make is to push away others in need of someone. Even as we desire meaningful relationships, somehow we neglect the ones who may need us the most. It hurts to be rejected by someone you hoped to bond with, let alone to feel as though every person you turn to doesn't want you around. I would say everyone has experienced feeling lonely or unaccepted at some point in their life, so why would we ever push others away?

Now, I understand that no one is perfect, and mistakes will be made—but we must stop dividing ourselves as a culture. If everyone struggles, why do we cast out individuals for their mistakes or flaws as if we do not have any ourselves? It does not matter how amazing someone is, people will find something to criticize. Jesus Christ was the only perfect human that walked this Earth, and even He was betrayed, tortured, and slain.

When people distract themselves from their own flaws by focusing on another's, they are searching for false confidence within themselves rather than being who God made them to be. It may seem more pleasing to distract yourself with someone else's issues rather than focusing on your own, but this is just prolonging the inevitable. At some point, we each have to face our own issues.

DON'T BE AN ENABLER

As horrible as it is to push away the individuals that need love, giving attention to the ones that are causing harm is just as sinister. There should be nothing attractive to anyone about someone who enjoys ignoring or hurting others. "Joking" with people about a topic that causes them pain is unacceptable, and we need to shift our values from casually hurting others to bringing everyone together. It is becoming more and more difficult to find someone of generous heart. *You* must be the individual with a compassionate heart and a positive outlook to be a light in the world around you.

But just as you shouldn't enable those around you to act dishonorably toward others, don't allow it in yourself, either. Talking negatively about people that you choose to view as beneath you only demonstrates your own insecurities and lack of character. The same goes for talking down to others as if you're better than them. When someone is confident in him or herself, there is no desire to hurt others' self-esteem and tear them down. Confident people raise up those around them because there is no satisfaction in witnessing pain in others. I am not saying that if you lack confidence, you will always put others down, or that if you are confident, you will always lift others up; however, hurting others to make yourself seem more attractive is an indicator of insecurity and demonstrates how mentally unhealthy you are.

Despite the state of your own suffering, lifting up others is fulfilling a positive purpose. When you have earned the respect of others as a positive role model, you must lead through example and choose kindness even when everyone around you is choosing negativity.

It takes zero courage to criticize someone's behavior without knowing what occurs in his or her life. Courage can be demonstrated through taking the time to understand someone, and attempting to discover why they make the decisions they do. Once you know someone well enough, you should privately speak to that individual to help without attracting attention to their issues. Understanding and helping someone in a private manner is respectful, and thus appreciated. Negatively speaking about other's behavior will not create any positive change, but privately helping and teaching those people will be one step towards establishing the positive impact this world needs.

BE THE CHANGE YOU WANT TO SEE IN OTHERS

Everyday you have a chance to be a positive impact. Before bed at night, think back through your day, assessing whether your actions were a positive or negative contribution to another person's life. You will either have a sense of satisfaction and confidence because you know that you worked hard or made a contribution, or you will experience the opposite. If you are doing something you know is wrong, then that sense of guilt or unhappiness will linger in the back of your mind. People may try to ignore their guilt, justify it, or do things to distract themselves from it. Causing harm to others causes harm to yourself as well. When people do not even want to be around you because of the way you treat others, you will feel empty and void of satisfaction. However, satisfaction and happiness can be facilitated through the positive energy you bring to the environment you are in.

My football coach was one of the greatest mentors I have ever had. He used to tell the team to imagine the way we speak to our teachers, and if we would want someone to speak that way to our parent. Before you speak negatively to or about anyone, imagine how you would feel if someone spoke to your family or someone you love in that way. It may not be your own mother that you are disrespecting, but it may be someone else's. Each time you treat someone disrespectfully, you are potentially speaking to someone's current/future wife, current/future husband, mother, daughter, son, father, brother, sister, etc. Do not ever treat someone that is loved by someone else in a manner you would not want someone you love to be treated.

SPEAK KINDLY, AND TAKE CHARGE OF YOUR EMOTIONS

Words have power, and are easily abused. As such, words are often brandished as weapons. Sometimes people don't even notice that their words are hurtful, because they're coming from a place of unchecked emotion. I have struggled with anger throughout most of my life, and I have felt as if I was not in control of my actions in certain circumstances. I used to get so filled with rage that I'd lash out over things I subconsciously understood were not worth becoming so emotional over. I was allowing myself to act based on emotions, damaging my relationships with those around me. I'd say ugly things I would later regret, and I discovered that the more I would react during my momentary anger, the more damage I was causing. I am not an anger management specialist, nor in a position where I can properly teach you exactly how to deal with your own anger or emotions, but I discovered what personally helped me. Over time, most of my anger diminished once I surrendered myself to God.

I am sharing my battles with you because I do not want you to hurt someone, as I have, by not taking control of your emotions. I have lost relationships with people that were very important to me because I did not know how to deal with the issue until it was too late. When in a negative situation, ask yourself these questions:

"Is this really that big of a deal?"

"What is the best way to handle this?"

Then take action, if necessary. But do not allow your temporary emotions to permanently damage relationships with people you care about. Be cautious with what you say, because we're not always aware of how great an impact our words can have on someone else.

ASSUME THE SURFACE DOESN'T TELL THE WHOLE STORY

We usually don't have a complete understanding of the suffering someone else may be going through. Only God fully understands the internal battles we face. Humans can incorrectly perceive someone to be happy while they're secretly in the throes of depression, which can be disguised by the most beautiful smiles. How are we to know by the surface alone?

I have dealt with cruelty and humiliation at the hands of others, because no one knew what I was going through. Their lack of knowledge influenced their desire to put me down—but it shouldn't have made any difference at all. It is so important that we empathize, listen, and support those around us as best we can.

When I was placed in the foster system, I began to meet other foster children in my area. I discovered that I recognized more of them than I expected, and some I never would have guessed were foster kids. Most of these children were damaged and emotionally scarred, but they could also be extremely loyal, kind, and generous. It was inspiring to see the resilience of the human soul, that these kids could go through so much pain and yet still be so kind.

This experience taught me how unaware we can be of the secret pains of others, and it moved me to spread love and compassion to everyone I meet. The temporary feeling of empowerment that someone may experience because they put someone down does not compare to the satisfaction of knowing you expressed love to someone when they needed compassion. And people remember such acts of kindness more than accomplishments or social status.

Let's say that you achieve all your dreams and become very financially successful. Would you rather be remembered as the person who has wealth and popularity, or the person who impacted lives by reaching out to the broken? Both may sound appealing, but only one will bring true satisfaction and happiness. During a dark time in someone's life that we may not be aware of, our actions could determine everything for them. Since we cannot always know of the pain someone is facing, we *can* realize the potential of our actions to save someone's life—as well as end it.

FEED LIGHT, NOT DARKNESS

There is so much negativity and darkness in this world, which is why we need more people to shine a light. I have discovered that no matter my struggles, easing someone else's pain always helps me confront my own. And doesn't it feel great to help someone in need, friend? Fun fact: it releases a hormone called dopamine within our brain, which is a chemical that makes us feel pleasure. It gives us a high, and can be addicting, in a sense. I love when people tell me that I have inspired or helped them through something just by sharing my story. I do not, however, think it makes me better than anyone else. I love it because I understand what it is like to go through tough times and feel all alone. I sincerely enjoy witnessing others finally overcome their own battles.

There have been holidays when I didn't get much in the way of gifts, and it was blamed on becoming a man. I found it hard to be happy in those conditions because it seemed as if all my friends were getting whatever they wanted. I do not believe I would have the love for giving that I do, or as much appreciation for what I have, if not for my experiences in having so little. If you have been blessed with people in your life that have always been there to provide you with the things you need and desire, then you are more fortunate than you realize.

Imagine a society where everyone pulled each other up in

their most difficult times; no one was alone on holidays, no one went to bed hungry, or felt so isolated they wanted to end their own life. Aren't such goals worth reaching for? The world may be full of various cultures that function differently, but in the end, we're not so different from one another. We all have hopes and dreams, struggles and fears, and we all "bleed the same".

DON'T THINK LESS OF YOURSELF—THINK OF YOURSELF LESS

Sadly, the main reason that unity seems so unattainable is because each new generation is becoming even more focused on themselves than the one before. But hear this: it does not matter how "cool" or successful you are, because neither determine true character. If you measure value or importance as a human being based on personal accomplishments, finances, or social status, your perspective is entirely shallow and perpetuates a faulty mindset.

As we gain new life experience, our values and perspectives tend to drastically change over time. Whatever may be making you feel better about yourself now may not have the same effect on you later on. For example, money and social status can only provide the feeling of happiness for so long before they become old hat and are no longer enough. But if I were to die today, knowing that I helped as many people as possible while I had the chance, I'd be okay with that. The more you focus on your own petty concerns, the more you hold yourself back.

Selfishness is part of human nature, it's true, and everyone is guilty of it at one time or another. But when selfishness is practiced, even without conscious effort, it becomes a habit in our lives.

It's a good thing we know habits can be changed with persistence and intention, huh?

This applies to me, too. I feel pity for myself sometimes, or forget to consider another person's viewpoint in a disagreement. But selfish thinking, left unchecked, leads to self-destruction. We tend to avoid looking outside our own perspective when we're too far submerged into our own lives. Is it challenging not to constantly focus on ourselves? Of course. However, once you develop a habit of putting yourself in others' shoes and thinking outside yourself, your mind will grow, as will your relationships.

EXPAND YOUR SCOPE OF VISION

As a teenager, I can attest to the common assumption that "it will never happen to me", whatever "it" is. This mindset stems from a lack of life experience. Do you think Toothless Joe, the homeless man on the corner, planned to become homeless? Do you think my dad sat in his seventh grade classroom penning essays on his future as a drug addict? I did never considered the idea that I would eventually be enrolled in the foster care system, but it happened.

It's easy to grow accustomed to any life when you've lived it long enough. It's easy to forget that each and every choice leads you down a path to a future you can't see yet. Yours could be hanging by a thread right now—but you won't see it if your focus only extends to the tip of your nose.

So shift. Expand your scope of vision. Realize how fortunate you are. Choose to share your blessings with others who have less, because wouldn't you want that if your roles were reversed? After all, you never know—one day, they *could* be. Whatever you have to offer, imagine sacrificing just one day of your life to go around the community and help people as many people in need as you can, possibly changing lives. Imagine if every single person in America did this, for just one day. The improvements, the happiness spread, would be colossal!

And it starts with just one person. One individual who intentionally goes out to make that difference in their community.

One person to lead by example.

The bottom line is this: your actions have more of an effect on the people around you than you realize. Most people are not leaders, but followers, waiting for someone around them to light their way. Once you step out in a way that is completely different than everyone else, people will notice, and possibly follow.

Be the spark that creates a positive change, my friend.

BE GENUINE

Authenticity and being true to one's word are not attributes that today's society puts much stock in (despite the numerous ad campaigns and platform slogans you may encounter that pretend otherwise). It's an epidemic, in fact. Why tell the truth when you can lie?

But there is nothing respectable about someone who is not true to what they say. Who wants to be close to someone with the reputation of a liar?

I've mentioned before that words have power. Even so, anyone can flap their jaws. And as easy as it is to speak, it's equally easy to tell a lie. This is why actions are so much better than words when it comes to discerning authenticity. Actions are a demonstration of someone's true nature. As words say one thing, actions speak louder, making it far more difficult to hide one's true identity behind them.

ACTIONS VS. WORDS

I understand that people's actions may give a false sense of honor or love, just as words can. Honestly, nothing is guaranteed. There is not an exact method you can apply to be able to discover someone's real intentions. But truth eventually finds its way to the surface. When people prove themselves as trust-worthy to you, even through the tough circumstances, remember to appreciate them. My grandmother is someone I love and appreciate more than almost anyone; she is nowhere near perfect, but she has had my back through every negative situation, and her constant love and acceptance has been a huge blessing in my life.

While you should always be on guard against liars and manipulators, you should also guard yourself against becoming one. It's almost instinctual to apologize or try to justify ourselves after hurting someone, but an apology does not always heal what has been broken. No one is perfect, sure, and everyone makes countless mistakes in their life; but just as words have power, actions have more, and are therefore to be held to an even higher standard of accountability.

But both the best and worst of people know this is the way of things, don't they? I think it's why we are prone to giving insincere apologies—it's what we were taught to say, whether we mean it or not. It's expected, and we aren't let off the hook until B follows A. It's almost a cause-and-action checklist scenario: did something wrong, must apologize. Check.

Sometimes, a person that once hurt you may return and genuinely ask for your forgiveness. What should you do then?

I, for one, think people can change, but believe it or not, the offender's possible changing is irrelevant to your forgiving them. We should *always* forgive the people that hurt us—not for their benefit, but for our own freedom. Why? Because letting go of negative emotions and old wounds may be a very difficult and long process, but we should never allow someone that harmed us to have so much control over our lives. Forgiveness truly is freedom, because when we forgive, we are letting go of something that drags us down and holds us back.

I could be angry towards the people who have hurt me and continue to give them power over my life, or I can choose to let go of the past, and accept my situation in the present.

In the event that you're never offered an apology for being wronged, know that it's normal to desire closure, or to want to understand why that person did what they did to hurt you. But even the best closure will not fully heal the wrongs. Even if you were granted an opportunity to share with your offender the extent of your hurt, they may not care; or if they did, their guilt or regret would not alleviate your pain.

Acceptance and forgiveness are some of the most powerful weapons we can brandish against any obstacle we encounter. It is better to trust God and give our cares over to Him than try to carry our emotional baggage on our own. You cannot heal and grow from a situation if you are constantly dwelling upon the past. No one can both look in the past and embrace the future.

Furthermore, when someone repeatedly hurts you, yet you allow him or her to continue being part of your life, you are giving that person more opportunities to cause you damage. If someone apologizes and proves they truly meant it by way of demonstrating a change in their actions, you can trust that they will not continue making the same mistakes that hurt you.

Of course, mistakes will be made within a relationship of any kind—but someone's repetitive actions toward you demonstrate what you are worth to them. An apology without change is manipulation; do not allow yourself to be manipulated. You can hold out hope for a person to eventually change *without* putting yourself in danger of being hurt by them again.

MANIPULATION IS FOR JERKS

Manipulation is a powerful tool people often use to make you believe that their negative decisions were your fault. Most people attempt to avoid claiming responsibility for their mistakes and will try to place the blame on someone else. People will not only try to convince you that their actions were your fault, but they will convince themselves of this. It is extremely upsetting how sinister someone you love can be towards you, but not everyone is who they claim to be. Sometimes the person you love the most is the worst thing for you, but there is a reason for everything. It is often stated that "God gives the toughest battles to his strongest soldiers". The situations that make us think our life is destroyed and that our book is closing may only be occurring to open the next chapter.

If someone truly does love you, they will stick with you through thick and thin. Love is a permanent commitment, not a temporary feeling. Do not mistake my words to mean that people who love you should stick with you no matter your actions; there are situations in which you absolutely need to remove the people that are dragging you down. But if there is mutual authentic love, each person will want what is best for the other person. Love should not be a one-sided commitment where one person makes the other better while the other holds their loved one back.

People often stick with someone who is hurting them because they believe they will eventually become the person they desire them to be, or will return to who they used to be. People can change, but you cannot *make* them change. Change can only take place once someone decides it for themself. You are only holding yourself back if you are waiting on someone to change. People are who they choose to be, and only they are responsible for their character and actions.

PRETENDERS

Difficult situations will separate the people who are genuine from those who are merely putting on an act. When your life turns in a negative direction, the ones that love you will fight harder to stay there, while the pretenders distance themselves because they do not want your problems to affect them. Not everyone is with you because they love you or your heart; they may be there because they love something that you possess, or value something in which you bring to their life. There have been loved ones I would have given my life for in a heartbeat who ended up fighting the hardest to stay away from me. Although it was awful, their actions informed me of their true colors, which was something I needed to know.

When someone else's inauthenticity hurts you, use your pain as fuel to spread love rather than continuing the cycle of hurt. Creating a cycle of pain will not make you feel better, and damages other people. It can sometimes feel awkward or vulnerable to show others who you really are, but we should all be ourselves around everyone. Then once you spread authentic love to those around you, you will receive it in return.

As genuine people are becoming more difficult to find, the world needs more representation of what a genuine person is really like. If people want to cut you out of their life for being who you really are, allow it. Fake friends are always replaceable, but people that love you for you who you are is priceless and should be cherished. Whenever someone chooses to leave your life, remember that you are opening your life to more people that are searching for someone like you. Make room for those who really want to know you, and do not stress yourself over the people who do not.

A purge like this is much more healthy than people realize. You are not losing people so much as letting go of the negativity and fakeness they brought into your life. Sometimes it hurts or leaves us with a feeling of emptiness or uncertainty, but we need to be surrounded with people that bring positivity and joy into our lives. Every relationship takes two people, and not everyone will be as dedicated to you as you are to him or her. Do not push away the people that are fighting to be by your side, and remember that the people who did leave you chose that, so if anyone is missing out, it's them.

Today's society perpetuates a world of fakeness—fake news, fake poses in photos, fake plants on the windowsill, fake designer clothes, fake hair color. The list goes on. Sadly, we're all pretty determined to portray our lives better than they are. Almost everyone is on social media, showcasing a finely curated life according to what they want people to perceive about them. Social media is not a completely negative thing, but it is also not a representation of the real world. People love to hide their struggles behind the filtered facade of their social media accounts. Even knowing this, we *still* compare our real lives to the fake ones we see on social media, driving us to pour more fakeness into our own profiles for others to see. It's an ugly cycle of self-doubt for everyone.

These picture-perfect lies fed by social media are not attractive to me. I enjoy seeing the flaws in people because our imperfections are what makes us human. We live in a time where authenticity is fading away as people cling more and more to their fake, problem-free, virtual lives. It's natural to be attracted to this idea of perfection, but once we accept our flaws and let go of this fascination, we can learn to be happier, and to grow, despite anything that comes our way.

But yeah, I get it—it is obviously easier to follow the crowd. But you know what's much more rewarding? Being the leader. We each have a choice, every single day, to either help change someone else's life for the better, or to follow the path of everyone else. For example, it would have been easier for me to take the same negative direction as my family. Thankfully, because of my experiences, I chose a new road. I know what legacy I desire for myself, and the path I want to set for the future generations of my family. There is no true reward in idly following the path that was set for us; what is more rewarding is breaking down boundaries and chasing after something greater than ourselves.

YOU DEFINE YOU

Another aspect of being genuine involves being yourself, and not letting anyone else define or limit you outside of your identity in Jesus Christ.

I used to believe I was a victim, and my beliefs were reinforced through my own negative actions. I used to drag the people around me down, just a negative influence living for comfort and sin, too focused on what others thought of me. I knew in the back of my mind that the way I was acting was not the genuine version of myself, but I needed an internal change. I was so desperately eager to please and be respected that I was losing not only my morals, but all the good qualities that make me the person I am.

The way I was living did not leave me with true satisfaction or happiness. I felt temporary excitement, but I knew deep down that my actions weren't good for me or anyone around me. Once I straightened up my act, I became so much more fulfilled. Being a genuine and positive leader for your community is always more exciting than being a blind follower.

You may be thinking to yourself that you desire to make a positive change, but you do not know where to begin. A great place to start is looking within yourself. The energy you give off affects the people around you more than you think, so allow your presence to be so positive that it's contagious to everyone around you. I believe that when you are a Christian, your faith can be demonstrated through your actions and the way you present yourself. When God is the number one priority in your life, others will notice the fruits you bare. I am not stating my spiritual beliefs will be shared by everyone around me, but my positive energy can be.

We only have one life, so why not use it to make a positive impact? It does not matter if you change one person's life or a million, as long as you are making some sort of positive contribution. I, for one, refuse to be a negative force in this world. Life has knocked me down plenty of times, but all my pain and emotions will be channeled and used to contribute positively to the people in my realm of influence. The person you are is ultimately chosen by you and directed by God. Choose to be the truest version of yourself. Genuineness is difficult to find, so cherish and embrace everything that makes you who you are.

LOVE YOURSELF

One of the greatest gifts God has given mankind is individuality: those distinguishable characteristics that make us all different from one another, uniquely "us".

It's all too common to idolize others for their strengths and accomplishments while forgetting that they have their own flaws. We must validate and use the strengths God has given us as individuals, or what good are they?

A great example of why differences are so vital within a society can be seen in a football team. A team composed of all the best quarterbacks in the world would not be successful because every player would only be good at one position. A football team depends on the diversity of its players. In order to dominate their opponents, the team needs players that are big, strong, fast, small, and wide, and each player on the field must adhere to their one assigned role, working together to contribute to the team's overall success. And if any one position were not to be filled, the weak spot would be immediately felt in the first play of the game.

Isn't that a good reminder that everyone's life has purpose? All strengths can be played upon to contribute to this world and make a difference. Even if you have not reached your full potential yet, use the gifts God has given you. No matter where you are in life, you have the potential to fill an important role.

And everyone starts somewhere, friend. Never forget this: our current situation does not determine our possibilities. If someone else has accomplished something, we have the capability to accomplish it as well. Our potential is only limited by our own mental barriers, such as a lack of faith in God or lack of faith in ourselves.

And you'll do well to also remember that achievement without accomplishment happens all the time. Even the most successful person in the world may not feel fulfilled at the height of their achievement.

We tend to criticize ourselves because of how little we have gained in comparison to someone else. It does not matter what airs a successful person may give off—no one has everything figured out. Do not mistake someone's worth as more than your own, especially when you may not be able to see what's really going on within that person. The traits you may wish you had, someone else may secretly hate about him or herself. The things you wish you could get rid of, someone else may crave to obtain. Remember that our differences are what make us unique, but that's not all of who we are.

I have considerable life experience for someone my age, and I love the Lord; however, I'm far from perfect. I am scared to love, trust, or open myself up to people because I have a fear of abandonment. I know love and its associated feelings require being vulnerable, but I am afraid of that vulnerability. I am extremely thankful for the people that God has brought into my life, but allowing new people in and inviting them to share an intimate portion of my world can be difficult for me. I have numerous flaws and insecurities, and I have made countless mistakes—but I will not hide them from the rest of the world just so people can think I'm more put-together than I am. Even when we're constantly trying to improve ourselves, we must learn to accept who we are at all stages of development.

I can dwell on my past regrets all I want, but they won't change. We must develop an understanding of the things we can improve, and what we must accept. I know it can be difficult, but in order to be happy, each of us must learn not to focus on the past or the qualities we are not capable of changing.

The shape of our physical bodies is an example of something we may not currently be comfortable with, but we can work towards improving it. Yet even as you're working to improve, do not punish or become angry with yourself over your flaws. Self-hatred does you no favors.

BE OKAY WITH BEING ALONE

Turning away from self-hatred and developing a sense of self-love is so important because we cannot truly love someone else until we learn to love ourselves. When we depend on someone else for love rather than ourselves and God, we set ourselves up for failure. Everyone you love will eventually disappoint you because there is no such thing as a perfect relationship. Love and disappointment go hand-in-hand, actually. When we choose to build a foundation upon one human being's love and acceptance, we consequently become less capable of handling their shortcomings, causing extra damage. When we learn from God how to love ourselves and not be reliant upon individuals, we have a stable foundation, and can properly love someone else amidst their own journey of self-discovery.

The point is, love should not be a foolish reliance upon

flawed individuals because that will lead to hurt and frustra-tion. Sometimes it takes losing important relationships to build a foundation that will last. Reliance is imprisonment, while self-love is freedom.

One of the biggest mistakes I ever made was becoming reliant on a girl. She took the place of a woman figure, which I craved to have in my life. I idolized her, and believed she was the only thing I'd ever need. During the year and a half of our relationship, I thought we'd be together forever. I forgot how young we were. She had an amazing family, friend group, and an emotional foundation that made her less reliant upon me than I was on her. Our histories were nothing alike, so there was no void for her, no reason to latch onto me the way I had to her. She became such an idol that I turned away from God, in a sense, because I chose to rely on her more than Him.

We both grew and changed throughout our relationship, but we did not continue growing together. Once she left me, I had an intense feeling of emptiness and loneliness that was caused from unresolved issues in my past and not truly loving myself or God.

As painful as it was to lose her, it was one of the best things that could have happened to me in that time. I needed God to break my heart in order to destroy what was breaking His.

In my ensuing period of sadness, I discovered what a common mistake it is to rely on another person for happi-ness. People everywhere are searching for another human to take away their pain rather than turning to God, the only form of never-ceasing love and strength there is. We long for love so much that we settle into relationships because we're lonely, or because we think it will solve our problems. While a relationship can be a tremendous blessing, it's not a cure-all. Your demons will still find and haunt you. Discover how to love yourself better, and allow God's love to uphold you in the midst of turmoil.

BUILD YOUR CONFIDENCE

When you're in a recovery phase, it's helpful to work through your pain toward your goals. Try working out, writing, spending time with friends, and just overall rediscovering who you are. For me, the realization of how much I had not yet discovered about myself once I stopped spending all my time with one person blew my mind. I had to lose a love substitute in order to gain a true love for myself, and build a new foundation upon Christ.

I decided to join my high school football team, it gave me a new sense of confidence that I had never seen in myself before, and grew my character in numerous ways. The team became my new comfort zone, while my teammates and coaches became my family. I believe that football is what saved me from much of my pain because it was one of the ultimate tools for restoring confidence and growth. The head coach of our football program at the time was one of the greatest mentors I have ever had in my life, and I highly respect him to this day. He treated everyone on the team equally as men. The sport in general was a man's game where you would either fight to destroy your opponent, or you would lay down and lose. There was not a place for excuses or weakness, only courage and work ethic.

Whatever activity you choose, finding something that builds your confidence is necessary for getting through the tough times because it helps you take back control. Working out, playing sports, making music, dancing, singing, debating, working a job, helping others, spending time with people that you love—these are all activities that can boost your confidence and increase your level of happiness. Confidence is power, so learn how to acquire and apply it helpfully.

RAISE YOUR STANDARDS

One of the absolute best ways to obtain confidence is to raise the standards in every aspect of your life, starting with your relationship with the Lord. Refuse to allow yourself to settle for just anything that comes your way; only accept the best from yourself, and look for the best in everything around you. Do not settle with your friends, spouse, grades, income, or *anything* that plays into your well-being. Set the standards so high that the negative people will either stay away from you because they are intimidated by your level of achievement, or are drawn closer because they are intrigued by the difference they see in you.

The biggest difference between a straight A student and a student that is failing is his or her standards. A student that fails will accept failure and continue to fail, while a student with a 4.0 GPA will not accept getting a grade lower than their standards. One student is typically not smarter than the other, but one student has the bar raised higher. If you are a student reading this, write down and commit to the GPA you want to earn and do everything you can to achieve it. Your grades may not be very important to you, but they reflect your standards and work ethic.

The previous example relates to more than just grades, too. Your physical body, income, relationships, relationship with God, and many other things are all reflections of your standards and worth ethic. It is very easy to just accept what is being given to you, but it is not rewarding if it does not require effort. I am sure you have heard the saying, "if it was easy, everyone would do it". Doing what is perceived as "hard" is often not actually hard—it's just hard *enough* to make lazy people decide it isn't worth doing. Once you raise your standards and make a habit of taking a more challenging path, your life will change. You will begin to enjoy doing what is hard, and will fall in love with the process as much as the results.

TAKE CARE OF YOURSELF

When you love yourself, taking care of yourself is vital. I'm not talking about buying materialistic things or finding distractions, but participating in activities that will improve your life and character. Love yourself enough to only accept the best from yourself, nothing less.

Also understand that you do not need everyone's approval. I believe that if Jesus died for my sins and loves me despite my many mistakes and imperfections, then shouldn't *I* love me? Once you learn to love yourself as He loves you, happiness and self-love come much easier. God grants the strength to move forward from past mistakes and overcome hard times, and He has shown me that He has a greater plan for my life than I deserve in and of myself.

Satan works against God's people, fighting to tear down those being used by God to fulfill His purpose. Satan wouldn't waste time to destroy a person that is not interfering with God's plan, right? There have been times when everything was going great in my life, then something would happen to tear my happiness down. I used to be angry with God for allowing those things to happen, but now I realize my trials only reflect His confidence in me.

I want to use my past heartaches to glorify God, ultimately achieving His plan for me. No matter what we go through, we must love ourselves the way He loves us, and believe in ourselves the way He believes in us, while we trust Him with all things.

EXECUTION

(UN)MOTIVATION

I know that we all experience days where it seems nearly impossible to get out of bed. Sometimes we ache to just take some time off from our goals and relax, which is understandable. There is nothing wrong with feeling slightly unmotivated for a time; in fact, I have never met anyone who has not experienced a lack of motivation at some point.

The issue occurs when you never feel motivated and are constantly searching for comfort. You must conquer this laziness! It would be unrealistic to assume that you will never feel unmotivated ever again, but you still have the choice to adapt and overcome, to execute despite your momentary feelings.

Understand that if we truly desire something, we must outwork whoever else is out there working towards the same dream. In football, there may be ten different players competing for one starting position. The way to get the spot is through outworking the rest of the players competing with you. Coaches love to see hard work, and usually respect the players with hard work ethic. So the bottom line is this: you are not going to get the starting spot you want in your life if you do not outwork your competitors.

Forming a new positive habit or making an extreme change does not happen in one day. It requires self-discipline to give up whatever may be holding you back, and serious results will not occur until you are able to repeatedly follow through with your new actions.

SELF-DISCIPLINE

I had to become familiar with self-discipline and hard work around age thirteen. One of the qualities I have always strongly admired about my dad is his intense work ethic. He was never the type of man to make excuses for why he could not get the job done, and he always found a way to accomplish whatever he was asked to do. Once I moved in with him, I had to develop the same type of work ethic in order to provide myself with basic necessities, such as school shoes or clothes. At one instance, I had to sand nearly the entire inside of a house and paint multiple rooms in one work day. I found myself enjoying working with him because I was learning new skills, practicing a better work ethic, and earning a sense of accomplishment.

Once you have the perspective to enjoy doing what is hard, you're on your way to success. Laziness does not contribute towards anything good; in fact, your lack of action is contagious to the individuals around you, so you are, in essence, holding them back.

Even if you work just enough to sustain and support yourself, your laziness is still negatively affecting the people around you. In my various living situations growing up, I could have chosen to be lazy and simply accept the acts of kindness towards me and move on with my life, or I could work to put myself in a position where I could repay those acts one day. I want to work hard enough to pay back all the people that helped me through my hard times, and remind them that those acts were not unappreciated.

If you come from a background where struggling is very common amongst the people you love, there should absolutely be no place for laziness in your life. It is selfish to allow the people you love to continue struggling, while your focus is primarily on enjoying yourself and being entertained. Our disadvantages are some of our greatest advantages because we have the power to turn them into a drive for our success. If your family goes through a negative cycle and your primary focus is comfort, you will not establish a positive lifestyle for the generations in your family that come after you. Even if you're personally unfamiliar with financial struggle, there should still be no room for laziness because it equates to a lack of gratitude.

LET OTHERS INSPIRE YOU

If you simply cannot find motivation to work towards a good future for yourself, consider the people that you love. Are you willing to work towards supporting those that have been there for you? For example, my grandmother is one of my favorite people. She has done so much for me, but she struggles to pay the bills, and her children are not in a position to support her. She may not consider it this way, but I feel as if I should be the one to support her so she doesn't have to work until the day she dies. Whenever I feel lazy and not up to focusing on executing the plans I have set for myself in view of my goals, I think of her.

Think of someone in your life that you love and appreciate, possibly someone who has supported you in one way or another. How do you want to repay that person? What can you do now in order to change that person's life in the future? Once your drive is no longer focused on yourself, but rather someone else, your lack of motivation will depreciate. It can be hard to stay committed to something that we only want in order to benefit our own lives, but pushing to become greater versions of ourselves for someone else could be the key ingredient to making the difference.

People often dream up what they'll do or have once they accomplish a goal, but then they give up during the process of getting there because their goal does not proceed as smoothly or quickly as they hoped. The benefits we desire to see will not always happen right away. We must be committed enough to the process that we persevere until the end. And when your drive is based on how changing someone else's life, your commitment will be harder to break because it's no longer a self-focused desire.

One of the motivations that keeps me driven more than anything else is suffering. I have dealt with anxiety, loss, shame, uncertainty, and almost every negative feeling I can think of. Since I understand what it's like to deal with those feelings, I want to use my experiences to help end someone else's suffering to the best of my ability. It is hard for me to relax and enjoy myself while knowing millions of kids out there are going through experiences similar to what I went through. I empathize, and can't stop thinking about using my story as a platform to possibly teach them how to get through their own situations. The potential number of people I could help makes me not want to do anything except execute a plan to do just that. The pain in this world elevates my drive to a higher level because of my personal knowledge of what those experiences are like.

DISCOVER USEFUL OUTLETS

There may be people reading this who have never dealt with anxiety, but anxiety for me seemed as if my mind was battling against my heart every second, and I was constantly wrestling my own thoughts. It was in the midst of such battles that I discovered how anxiety magnifies what is in your heart, and how it can be very challenging to change what rules our hearts. I had a lot of negative thoughts, mainly from dealing with loss and feelings of abandonment, that I was unsure how to handle.

Anxiety is almost like getting punched in the stomach by your own thoughts when you least expect it. I fought my hardest not to allow them to take over my life and stop me from being happy, but all the negative emotions and thoughts carried over into my dreams, until eventually falling asleep was a struggle in itself. I am sure many of you can relate to such feelings from some point in your life, especially if you have gone through something very painful. The only thing that allowed me to overcome my anxiety was trusting in God, and turning those feelings into a drive for success and betterment—betterment of myself, those around me, and the world at large.

I became sick and tired of being scared to go to sleep and just lying in my bed at night, miserable. I decided to find some way to chase after my dream of helping people while also redirecting my thoughts. I began writing this book, and it honestly helped me overcome a lot. It was not only a step in the direction of achieving my goals, but also gave me an outlet to discharge my negative emotions.

It's okay if writing a book isn't the best outlet for you—do whatever you possibly can to embrace who God has shaped you to be. Make goals towards something positive to distract your thoughts and grow as an individual. I previously explained how being alone can be a good thing in order to evaluate situations and provide time to focus on ourselves, but Satan can also use isolation to try to destroy us.

YOU DON'T HAVE TO BE AWESOME

I believe that hard work and trusting in God are the best treatments for any negative situation. If you want to give yourself a better life or make your dreams into a reality, you must be willing to work hard—repetitively. However, as rewarding as hard work may be in the long run, it is even more rewarding if you choose to take a risk in the process. Be better than just living in your comfort zone and never growing as an individual because of the fear to explore new opportunities. There are not many things more rewarding than taking a risk and the risk turning out to be successful.

You may think it strange, but one of the greatest gifts God has given me is that I'm not amazing at one certain thing, but have the ability to be decent at almost anything I attempt. I may never become the smartest student, best athlete, or most accomplished speaker/author, but I have the potential to become fairly good at whatever I decide to do. Excelling in school does not come naturally to me as it does for some of my friends. Nonetheless, I still work hard on my education. It may not be my intelligence that will get me academic success, but if it's my work ethic, I'm okay with that. I will never be the smartest student, but I am able to control my work ethic to a point where it is difficult to compete against me in whatever I choose to do, which is largely because I will take risks to succeed. There are many extremely well-rounded and talented people with a great work ethic, but too many of them have not fully discovered themselves and all their talents because they fear the unfamiliar, rarely leaving their comfort zone.

TAKE RISKS

In a way, the circumstances of my life taught me how to lean into taking risks, as well as how to step out of my comfort zone. I have had to make many decisions on my own, and I never knew if I was making the right decision or ruining my life. It was a risk for me to decide to leave my mom's home, who I lived with for the first twelve years of my life. I took a risk to go back to my mom's later when I already knew how things played out the first time. I took a very big risk when I got on a plane back to Louisiana and was unsure where I would be living. I never had the slightest idea where my decisions would lead me. I could only hope for the best and act based off what seemed most practical for me under the current circumstances. However, the risks I took paid off because I am happier than I have ever been.

I have made many mistakes along the way that I am not proud of, but I believe that I am in one of the best possible situations I could be in, and I am certain there are amazing prospects ahead of me. Despite my failures, I refused to stay down and allow life to destroy me.

Never be afraid to take risks, or to fail. If you want to become an author, start a business, quit that job that makes you miserable, or whatever you believe that you are called to do, get out there and do it. I am not giving you an excuse to be unrealistic or to have no plan of execution, but never be afraid of failure. No matter what adversity you face, if you grow and learn from it, it can become a helpful experience.

Because the greatest advantage is a disadvantage.

Overcomers use their disadvantages to gain wisdom and determination, and then build on it to become the greatest versions of themselves. No matter what occurs on your personal journey, make the most of this precious opportunity called life!

ACKNOWLEDGMENTS

The journey of creating this book seemed as if it was an endless process and consisted of countless hours of hard work and persistence. Despite the effort I gave to this project, it would not have been possible if not for the amazing people in my life that assisted me. I am beyond thankful for God and everyone that has helped me along my journey. I have many blessings—friends and loved ones, old and new, people I've encountered through every phase of life that have let me lean on them as I stumbled along. I do not know where I would be without these individuals.

Everyone I spoke about in this book helped grow me, and moved me toward my future in some way. But first, I would like to recognize each family that helped take care of me throughout my journey.

This book exposed some of the flaws and mistakes made by my birth family, but I'd be lying if I said they didn't help me become who I am today. I appreciate them for that reason. My father and I are now very close and he is one of my biggest supporters. He is a hard-working and passionate individual, and I believe that I am a reflection of him in many ways. My mother and younger brother were also each such important factors in my life, and I will always remember the times my mom did everything she could to provide me with shelter and proper meals. I discussed the incidents that caused me to be forced out of her home, but I continue to love her and remember all that she did for me throughout my childhood.

If it was not for the Armstrong family, God only knows where I would have ended up. I had no place to live when the family decided to take me in and treat me as one of their own. My friend's mother, Holli Armstrong, is one of the hardest-working and caring women that I have ever met. She provided for me during times when I had no one else, and I will forever express my appreciation towards her and her parents, who assisted her in supplying me with the life of a normal child to the best of their ability.

Living with my current foster family was perhaps the largest adjustment of all for me, but this book would not exist if not for them. Each of my foster parents were heavily involved in the editing and revision process. They support me in numerous ways and I am beyond thankful they brought me into their home. The family also connected me to a fantastic author, Baj Goodson. Baj is the author of *Wall of Crosses*, which I highly recommend checking out! She patiently helped me create my cover, as well as guided my process of becoming a self-published author.

I'm thankful as well for the impact of several mentors in my life that have supplied me with wisdom and taught me many valuable life lessons. Billy Hankins is a man that married his way into the Armstrong family, and many of the lessons I discussed in the book came from him. I strive to demonstrate the amount of wisdom to others that he has shared with me. I would like to recognize my previous foot-ball coach, Brett Beard. Coach Beard helped grow my character as a young man, and reminded me that the cycle of my family does not define who I am, or my future.

There were many others that were part of my journey, and I am thankful for everyone that is or once was in my life because I would not change a single thing about my past.

And to you, reader: I really hope this book changed you even just a little as a person, and that it allowed you to grow your perspective on life and the value of difficult situations. If this book helped develop your character or helped you over-come a difficult obstacle, please share it with someone else that is dealing with their own struggles. Do not exist on this Earth to merely make an impression, rather help me create an impact!

Thank you for reading this, and thank you for your support!

ABOUT THE AUTHOR

TOMMY SIGMAN II is a fifteen-year-old student, speaker, and author. After entering the foster care system at age thirteen, he developed his experiences into a platform to encourage and challenge others in difficult situations. He lives outside of Baton Rouge, Louisiana. You can find Tommy at his website, tommysigman.com, and across social media on Facebook and Instagram.

CPSIA information can be obtained
at www.ICGtesting.com
Printed in the USA
BVHW072110310722
643480BV00001B/65

9 781734 390704